BARRY SHEENE

Bloomsbury Sport
An imprint of Bloomsbury Publishing Plc

50 Bedford Square
London
WC1B 3DP
UK

1385 Broadway
New York
NY 10018
USA

www.bloomsbury.com

BLOOMSBURY and the Diana logo are trademarks of Bloomsbury Publishing Plc

First published 2017
Foreword and supplied copyright photographs © Estate of Barry Sheene 2017
Text © Rick Broadbent
Captions © Phil Wain

British Library Cataloguing-in-Publication Data
A catalogue record for this book is available from the British Library.

Library of Congress Cataloguing-in-Publication data has been applied for.

ISBN: Print: 978-1-4729-4458-0
ePDF: 978-1-4729-4456-6
ePub: 978-1-4729-4459-7

2 4 6 8 10 9 7 5 3 1

Design by D.R. ink
Printed and bound in China by RR Donnelley Asia Printing Solutions Limited, Dongguan, Guangdong

Bloomsbury Publishing Plc makes every effort to ensure that the papers used in the manufacture of our books are natural, recyclable
products made from wood grown in well-managed forests. Our manufacturing processes conform to the environmental regulations of
the country of origin.

To find out more about our authors and books visit www.bloomsbury.com. Here you will find extracts, author interviews, details of
forthcoming events and the option to sign up for our newsletters.

BARRY SHEENE

The Official Photographic Celebration of the Legendary Motorcycle Champion

Rick Broadbent

with Phil Wain

B L O O M S B U R Y
LONDON · OXFORD · NEW YORK · NEW DELHI · SYDNEY

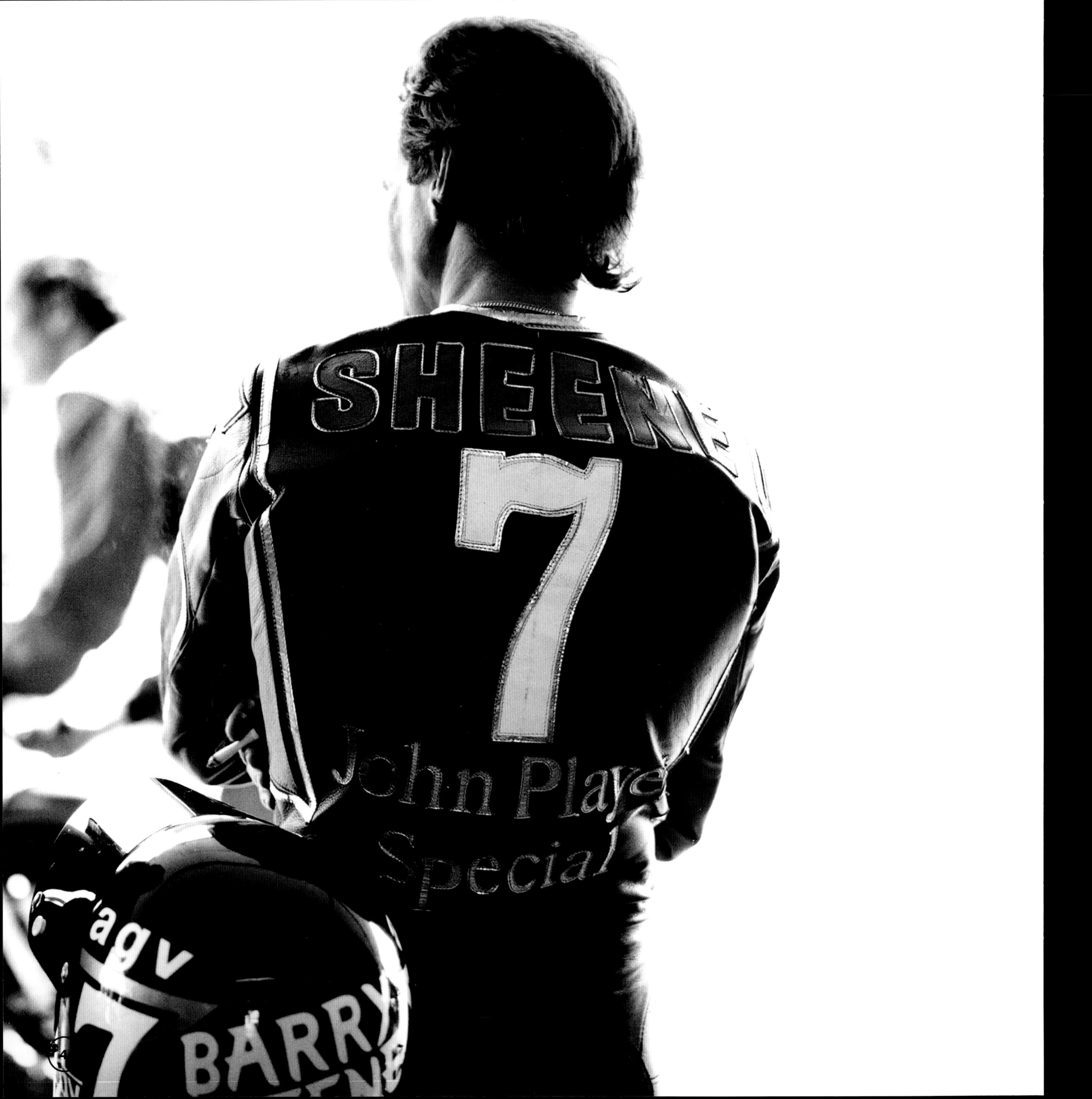
SHEENE
7
John Player
Special
agv
7
BARRY

CONTENTS

◄ The familiar number '7' was always emblazoned
on the back of Barry's leathers and was a sight
many of his rivals got used to seeing.

FOREWORD BY FREDDIE SHEENE

Everyone has their own memories of Barry Sheene. To bike-racing fans he was a superb rider, twice World Champion and insightful TV commentator. His fellow riders appreciated having him around the paddock for his sense of humour and invaluable technical advice, while the general public loved the charmer, the iconic playboy who had an innate sense of fun. To me he was all of these, but he was also my hero – and my dad.

Dad retired from racing and moved to Australia's Gold Coast a few years before I was born, but bikes were always going to be part of our lives. He got his first bike at the age of five and I did, too. In fact, I'd only just started at school when he allowed me to ride a little Yamaha PeeWee 50, the same one he'd used as a pit bike throughout his racing career.

For a few years I rode that bike every day after school, but even though Dad was constantly tinkering about in the garage to make it faster for me, I eventually outgrew the 50cc. It was 15 or more years old, the plastics had never been changed and I was eager for something shinier and faster. However, Dad never handed us anything on a plate. Even if it was a few coins for the sweet shop, it would always involve a challenge or a test.

◀ Tired, exhausted and yet clearly elated after a hard-fought victory at Le Mans, scene of the 1979 French Grand Prix. Barry Sheene was to grace the Grand Prix podium on an impressive 52 occasions throughout his career.

So Dad told me he'd buy me a new bike when I showed him I could wheelie the whole length of the garden on my PeeWee. If you're familiar with that bike you'll know it's practically impossible to do this on a machine with so little power, but I really wanted that new bike, so I set about trying to lift the front wheel, jerking it up as hard as I could. After much practice I believed I'd mastered it and called Dad down to prove I was up for the challenge.

As he stood watching, I readied myself for the great feat. Using a little rise in the ground, I pulled the front wheel up fiercely, but perhaps I was too desperate to succeed, because on my very first attempt I flipped the PeeWee, ripping the rear guard off, bending the handle bars back to the tank and breaking the throttle assembly. Dad, not unaccustomed to a messy crash himself, thought the whole thing was hilarious, but because I was so upset he went out and bought me my new bike. It was a Suzuki DS 80 – my first big bike.

One of the most exciting moments of my childhood was the delivery of Dad's new Agusta 109 helicopter, which he piloted himself. By this time I was a boarder at Geelong Grammar School in Melbourne. Dad picked me up from school and drove us to Melbourne airport. Together we flew the helicopter back up to the Gold Coast and he even let me take the controls as we flew 50 metres above the ocean or zig-zagged along the coastline. As a teenager, it was an incredible experience and although Dad's illness meant he could not fly as much as he would have liked, we did make a memorable trip together to watch the MotoGP

◀ Three generations line up for the camera with a young Freddie Sheene flanked by dad Barry and grandad Franco.

at Phillip Island, when Rossi went on to win the race.

Dad was a mix of everything you could ask for in a father. He was strict but fair, fun but serious. My sister Sidonie and I both had a cheeky streak – I wonder where that came from! – which quietly amused him. At times he indulged our naughtiness, posting us cigarettes at school or letting us have the odd drink, but despite nurturing a sense of mischief, he also kept us in check. If Mum told you he wanted a word in his office, you knew you were in trouble.

Sharing the legacy of Barry Sheene with the world is a privilege. Like any son, I look up to him as a role model and a father, but along with millions of fans I also respect what he achieved – his unique relationship with the public, his love for the sport and his incredible record as one of the greatest bike racers ever.

A slightly pensive looking Barry sits astride his Suzuki in the pits at Hockenheim, Germany, venue for the third round of the 1977 500cc World Championship. It was a textbook meeting for the Brit as he swept to pole position, the race win and the fastest lap of the race.

BARRY

It would be underselling Barry Sheene's appeal to hail him as a household name. He was also a sporting icon from palace to pub, a lovable rogue who mixed hair, flair and devil-may-care brilliance. In the 1970s he was as much a part of Britain as glam rock and the three-day week, and when Barry famously flicked a playful V-sign to Kenny Roberts during an epic 1979 Grand Prix at Silverstone it showed how this natural entertainer scarcely needed to lift a finger to forge his way into the public's hearts.

To be a truly household name you need to live beyond the narrow confines of your sport. So as well as the two 500cc world titles, Barry was the maverick who drilled a hole in his helmet so he could sneak a pre-race smoke; the 'bionic man' who came back from two mindboggling, and body-shaking, crashes; the Brut-splashing Jack the Lad who plundered life.

As time went on people likened him to George Best, sometimes dubbed the fifth Beatle and a star who mixed sport with women and drink and designer clothes. The comparison worked in terms of their shared appeal, both to legions of women and marketing men, but where there was a whiff of tragedy about Best, Barry refused to let anything beat him.

The miracle of his consummate 1976 500cc world title was that it came a year after he emerged from the mangled

◀ In the course of his career Barry won considerable silverware, garlands and accolades. The 1976 500cc Austrian Grand Prix was no exception: the talented Suzuki rider romped to victory.

He was the almost-cockney rebel who drove a Rolls-Royce but remained a blue-collar hero.

wreckage of his 175mph crash at Daytona, where he broke his leg, six ribs, his back, a wrist and his collarbone. When he came to in hospital the first thing he did was ask the nurse for 'a fag'.

As he fought back from his second news-making crash in 1982, he put a teaspoon up his rear to help his damaged bowel and proposed to Stephanie in a hospital toilet. It summed up the resilience and earthy romance of a man who had certainly never had a silver spoon in his mouth.

Barry was no saint and for every achievement like his 137mph record lap at the treacherous old Spa-Francorchamps circuit there was a TV thrown from a hotel window. He was the almost-cockney rebel who drove a Rolls Royce but remained a blue-collar hero.

Yet he was the purest of competitors. Freddie Spencer, twice a 500cc world champion himself, still remembers fondly that it was Barry who hugged him after his first GP win. Kenny Roberts once told me: 'I could not have had a greater rival when we went to battle.'

The TV adverts and hospital dinners sometimes masked the breadth of a rare talent. Barry had substance as well as style and knew how to develop a bike after years spent taking them apart with his father. He was a hands-on,

oily-fingered star who excelled in the wet and was jaw-droppingly brave.

He died too young, but lived at least two lives and his legacy endures. 'I loved Barry,' said Valentino Rossi, his natural successor as a champion showman. They had become good friends and Rossi met with Barry two months before he passed away. Rossi recalled, 'I think maybe he knew he was close to the end, but he said, "Come and have some fun."' And this wonderful private gallery of photographs shows Barry certainly had fun.

CHAPTER 1
BORN TO RACE

'Titles and trophies were waiting to be won, but I wasn't that ambitious at the time. The fun aspect of the sport took priority as far as I was concerned.' BARRY SHEENE

◀ The son of a former motorcycle racer turned experienced engine tuner, Barry spent his childhood travelling to various race meetings in the UK and Europe. The atmosphere was intoxicating and Barry openly admitted he grew up 'more interested in bikes than schoolwork': he used to skip class to watch practice sessions at Brands Hatch. The Donald Duck logo on his helmet first appeared in 1969 and Sheene openly admitted it was a bid to attract attention.

BORN TO RACE

There may have been something portentous about Barry Sheene growing up in a flat at the Royal College of Surgeons in London. Driven to succeed, he would ride to glorious and sometimes gory ends, his early years laced with the resilience that would one day see him crowned the greatest.

He was born to race. Father Frank, aka Franco, was the college's resident engineer and spent his spare time tuning motorcycles for the stars of '60s racing. His reputation led to a friendship and partnership with Francesco Bultó, founder of the Bultaco factory, and the opportunity for his son to ride good bikes in his nascent career.

That would spark some festering jealousy among Barry's peers, but it would be trite to suggest he ever had an easy life. After battling chronic eczema and asthma, the latter not helped by being a schoolboy smoker, he became an honest grafter who valeted cars, delivered antiques and filled bins to make money, working almost as hard as he played.

Some of those teenage exploits are legend, such as the carnal relations involving a church crypt and snooker table, but his pre-Stephanie reputation as a playboy was almost severed, quite literally, before he even made it

◀ Barry made his race debut at Brands Hatch in March 1968 aged just 17 in a club event. By all accounts his natural talent was obvious for all to see. His first win came at the same circuit, in just his second race meeting, and a mere two years after making his debut Sheene was crowned the 1970 125cc British Champion.

to school. A bath-time investigation of a toy train ended with the engine locked onto his nether regions, prompting screams and eventual freedom via Franco's bolt-croppers.

Franco's tools would continue to be a liberating outlet for Barry as he grew up. Variously described as difficult, cocky, precocious, obnoxious and, according to his sister Maggie, 'a little shit', Barry found his calling in the bike world.

It would not be a smooth passage, though. Authority always grated and the strictures of school were anathema to his independent spirit. Fights at his school off Trafalgar Square were common and even led to his first foray into the spotlight when his brawling saw him talent-spotted for the role of a hooligan at the nearby Royal Opera House. And so Barry Sheene, soon-to-be macho star of one of the grittiest of sports, played his role in Tosca, Puccini's tale of murder, torture and suicide, alongside one of the stage's great divas, Maria Callas.

His opera career was short-lived and he dispensed with school as soon as possible. Franco and Iris did little to dissuade their dilettante to stay on, giving him a note for the headmaster and £15 so he could travel to Europe for a month as spanner-man for American racer Tony Woodman. He was 14.

In the modern era, when boy racers are fast-tracked through race academies and lavished with premature sponsors, it seems barely believable. Motorcycle racing in the '60s was the sporting underbelly, with riders reasoning that three of them would be killed

each year and that they would each have six crashes. Hence they crossed off their spills and crossed their fingers. Part of Barry's legacy would be the way he propelled motorcycling towards the mainstream while championing greater safety.

Back then, though, he was a skilled back-up to successful GP racers such as Chas Mortimer, but determined Barry was never going to be content playing second fiddle. The first race came in March 1968 at Brands Hatch on one of his imported 125cc Bultaco bikes. He flirted with the lead before the bike seized and he crashed. Deploying that inveterate resilience, he ignored the shredded skin and aching head to get back on his 250cc bike and finish third in a second race. It was a typical triumph of bloody-mindedness over bloodied lip.

From the start Barry stood out. He had the Donald Duck logo and then his name on his helmet. White leathers would also be ordered. Hindsight is always 20/20, but he did not really need gimmicks to get on, even if they quickened the pace of publicity. From working for Mortimer, he was soon chasing Chas in the British 125cc Championship. He came second in 1969, but that was a year in which a man who seemed bereft of intimations of mortality wondered

From the start Barry stood out. He had the Donald Duck logo and then his name on his helmet. White leathers would also be ordered.

whether it was worth it. The reason was the death of Bill Ivy. The charismatic Kent racer, whose early 50cc bikes had been prepared by Franco, was killed in practice at the East German Grand Prix. His links with the Sheene family, and the fact that he was one of Barry's heroes for being fast and flamboyant, left Sheene pondering the point.

Racers rarely succumb to introspection for long. A year later a teenage Barry won the British 125cc title, and also made his Grand Prix debut in a one-off race in Spain, where he duelled with Angel Nieto before settling for second place. The Spaniard would go on to become

the greatest of all small bike racers, with 13 world titles, but the man who pushed him to the world title in 1971 was still living out of the back of a van and employing a suspect mechanic. 'He was the only one in the world who could not strip an engine, so I let him do the cooking while I did the mechanics,' Barry recalled. The friendship forged with Nieto in the heat of combat never wavered. Decades later, Nieto would tell journalist Nick Harris that Barry was the 'Valentino Rossi of his day'.

Barry's first Grand Prix win came at Spa that year, after he had been fined for spilling fuel on the track while returning from a late night out, and he might have won the 1971 world title had he not suffered broken bones

▶ Barry with the 250cc
Derbi at the Salzburgring,
Austria, in 1971.

in a non-championship race in Holland. He drew on his
resilience again by ignoring the broken ribs and bones in
his back to take Nieto to the wire.

Many of the enduring myths about Barry were created
in the time before he swung a leg over a 500cc Grand
Prix machine. His caravan was deemed luxury by the
grubby standards of the day, just as other riders would
grudgingly recall the white picket fence he had marking
out his space in the paddock. The truth was, Sheene
wanted better for men risking so much and actually
paved the way for others to ride on his coat tails.

Similarly, he is often damned for his negativity towards
the Isle of Man TT, but it is easy for those behind the

drystone walls to ignore more than 240 deaths on the Mountain Course. Barry went there in 1971 and crashed at Quarterbridge, but it is risible to suggest there were ever any half measures from a man who was so courageous around some of the world's most dangerous tracks, both at home and abroad. Later, Giacomo Agostini, TT legend and the most prolific Grand Prix winner of all, would join the chorus of disapproval without attracting anything like the criticism; Barry was always happy to be first and ever ready to speak his mind.

The yin and yang of a racer's lot saw a disappointing 1972 followed by the FIM Formula 750 European title in 1973. A year of reviving his image as the Next Big Thing came complete with domestic 500cc and Superbike titles. He was the King of Brands long before his star quality made him a commercial hit.

That was enough for Suzuki to hand him the RG500 and a ticket to the Big Show, the 500cc world championship, but his debut year was flawed and frustrating. As Phil Read beat Agostini in a battle of the old guard, Sheene was scarcely riding in the vanguard of change; he was again left wondering if it was all worth it when test rider and great friend Gary Nixon suffered a horrendous mid-season crash in Japan. Of course, he soldiered on to a distant sixth place in the title race.

If he thought he was through the storm, though, the resilience that had overcome toy train trauma and taped-up ribs was about to be tested like never before.

▲ Barry Steven Frank Sheene was born on 11 September, 1950. The Sheene family – dad Franco, mum Iris, older sister Margaret and baby Barry – lived in a four-bedroom flat in Holborn, London, which came with Franco's job as general maintenance man at the Royal College of Surgeons. It was a position he held for 40 years. Iris also worked at the college, as housekeeper, which meant she had the responsibility of cooking for all the visiting surgeons.

Sleep was never one of Barry's main attributes, as he continually scratched himself when lying down in his cot, keeping everyone else awake. He also suffered terribly with asthma until his teens, and a severe attack during the family holiday to the Isle of Man TT in 1955 saw him spend two days in Noble's Hospital.

His sister Maggie was actually born in Brighton after Iris was advised to move out of London due to the bombing dangers of the 1940s. Margaret eventually married Paul Smart, one of the UK's leading motorcycle racers of the 1960s and '70s.

'I was never a weedy, fragile-looking kid like some are with asthma ... I was as tough as any youngster of my age.' BARRY SHEENE

▲ Barry takes a ride on one of his dad's Bultacos. Sheene senior, Franco, was a keen racer, riding at leading UK meetings held at Brooklands, Blandford, Oulton Park and the Isle of Man. He retired in 1956 to spend more time with his family. He returned to the circuits during the 1960s, tuning 50cc and 125cc Bultaco machinery for a number of riders, including future World Champions Phil Read and Bill Ivy. When Franco raced, Barry would be with him, watching and learning. The two were inseparable. Years later, Franco would be ever-present with Barry in race paddocks all round the world.

▶ Barry was also well known for his mechanical prowess, having learned his skills at an early age from his father Franco. Aged only 14, Barry skipped school to spend a month in Europe as a Grand Prix motorcycle mechanic for American Tony Woodman. He would take a similar role in 1968 – this time for a full season, working with British racer Lewis Young. He could strip, fix and rebuild engines, something he'd picked up from Franco, who was not only a regular club racer but a wizard two-stroke tuner. Motorbikes played a big part in Franco's life and most of his evenings were spent in the workshops doing something connected with machines.

'The only subject at school I was top in was absenteeism.'
BARRY SHEENE

▲ Barry with his mum Iris enjoying an overseas family holiday.

▶ Barry gets a helping hand to push-start his Bultaco at a race meeting in March 1969. His racing career had got underway a year earlier and his debut outing at Brands Hatch was something of a baptism of fire: he came close to a fairy-tale win, only to crash out when his 125cc Bultaco seized. Undeterred by numerous cuts and bruises he went back out in the 250cc race 30 minutes later – nervous, excited and full of adrenaline – to claim an impressive third. Sheene's racing was firmly up and running.

Aged just 18, Barry soon became popular with fans of all ages. By the mid-1970s, he was comfortably the most popular British rider in the paddock, regularly staying behind after the races to sign autographs for his horde of followers.

'The reason I started
racing was to do
something at the
weekends.'
BARRY SHEENE

◄ Barry's early breakthrough came while riding the
125cc, 250cc and 280cc Bultacos tuned so expertly by
his dad, Franco, who had a long-standing relationship
with Senor Bultó, the owner of the Spanish manufacturer.
Barry's first full season of racing in 1969 in the 125cc
British Championship saw him battling with seasoned
campaigners, such as Chas Mortimer and Jim Curry, and
competing at the iconic race circuits Croft, Scarborough,
Castle Combe and, shown here, Oulton Park. Note Sheene's
determination to streamline his body for extra speed.

▲ Barry ended the 1969 season second overall in the 125cc British Championship, a close runner-up to Chas Mortimer. The season saw Barry take an impressive victory at Castle Combe. Mum Iris (second right) and dad Franco (third right) travelled to all of the race meetings and made a formidable support team. The following year, 1970, Sheene would win the 125cc British Championship.

▶ Barry posing with dad Franco. Together, they invested in a 125cc ex-works Suzuki twin cylinder, the bike that arguably transformed Barry's career. The bike cost the princely sum of £2000, a significant amount of money in 1970, and it wiped out the Sheene funds, both father's and son's. The pre-owned race bike had achieved a lot in the hands of former rider Stuart Graham and would give Barry two superb years of racing.

'My parents mean more to me than anything. I've never been spoiled but my parents have always been so understanding.' BARRY SHEENE

◀ Barry raced in the 1971 125cc World Championship, where he rode his own privately entered Suzuki. He also had a new 250cc twin-cylinder Derbi at his disposal, which he raced in the 250cc World Championship that ran simultaneously with the 125cc event.

The first time he raced the 250cc Derbi was in that year's inaugural Austrian Grand Prix at the Salzburgring. Despite a terrible misfire, which meant the engine was running below optimium capacity, he was lying in a strong second place when the engine finally expired. More seizures followed in subsequent meetings and his only 250cc World Championship points came when he took sixth at the Sachsenring circuit in East Germany. He would fair much better in the 125cc category.

▲ The luxuries of a factory-backed rider were a long way off, and it was a basic existence for the youngster Barry and his mechanic Don Mackay as they toured the 12, all-European, World championships venues in their van. 'There was enough money to buy fuel and the floor of an oily Transit van isn't the best place to get a good kip. We slept in two cold sleeping bags and ate like hippies, a can of baked beans one day, maybe a frugal salad the next.'

The World Championship season featured visits to Salzburgring (for the Austrian Grand Prix), Hockenheimring (German Grand Prix), Snaefell Mountain, Isle of Man (British Grand Prix), Assen (Dutch Grand Prix), Spa-Francorchamps (Belgian Grand Prix), Sachsenring (East German Grand Prix), Brno (Czechsolvakian Grand Prix), Anderstorp (Swedish Grand Prix), Imatra (Finnish Grand Prix), Dundrod (Ulster Grand Prix), Monza (Italian Grand Prix) and Jarama (Spanish Grand Prix).

'I was keen to show what I could do out there.'

BARRY SHEENE

▶ The 1971 125cc World Championship witnessed Barry (4) battle all year long with Spanish rider Angel Nieto (1) on the factory Derbi and, to a lesser degree, Italian Gilberto Parlotti (2) on a works Maico. Nieto won five races to Barry's three (the Belgian Grand Prix, Swedish Grand Prix and Finnish Grand Prix) while Barry scored the most points from 11 rounds, by 109 to 87. However, only the rider's best six results counted towards the World Championship and Nieto took the title by eight points (87 to 79).

◄ The ten-speed 125cc Suzuki may have been built in 1967, but when Barry raced in England in 1971, he would win the 125cc races nearly every time. He won the 125cc British Championship in both 1970 and 1971 and would almost certainly have won the 250cc title too in 1971 had he not opted to miss the final round at Snetterton in order to make his North American debut at a big money meeting in Ontario. British rider Steve Machin won the race at Snetterton and with it the title, leaving Barry in second.

▶ Barry relaxing in the paddock prior to a race. Racers competed in both the World Championship and British Championship simultaneously, meaning that they could compete in as many as 25 race meetings a year on a range of very difficult circuits, such as the 14-mile Nurburgring or the badly surfaced Imatra in Finland. The prize money would range from £200 to £2000. It was a dangerous business too, with as many as six riders losing their lives a year between 1968 and 1973, including famous riders Bill Ivy, John Hartle, Jarno Saarinen and Renzo Pasolini. Safety standards were rudimentary at best.

Barry raced the Bultaco in British Championship rounds because the Suzuki was far superior to what anyone else had — whenever he raced it, he had dominant wins. With the Suzuki being a 1967 machine, it was also getting harder, and costlier, to obtain spares, so Barry felt it was too precious to risk in UK races.

◄ A cheerful and confident Barry relaxes with Franco at the 1971 Isle of Man TT, following the 125cc race scrutineering. He'd enjoyed the TT as a young spectator and paddock helper, and was looking to score some valuable points for his 125cc World title campaign, having taken third in the opening Grand Prix of the year at Salzburgring. However, while dad Franco was an ardent supporter of the TT, Barry's happy mood soon changed, and what happened on the following days would see the start of a difficult relationship with the event.

▶ Barry led the 1971 125cc TT in the early stages until he hit thick fog over the Mountain and eased off. Experiencing clutch problems, he crashed out at Quarter Bridge at the start of the second lap. In his own words, 'The Mountain circuit didn't frighten me in any way. I just couldn't see the sense in riding around in the pissing rain completely on your own against the clock.'

▶ While Barry's dislike of the Isle of Man TT was well publicised, the opposite was true for his dad Franco, who loved the Mountain Course. He competed at the TT between 1950 and 1954, as well as at the Manx Grand Prix in 1955 and 1956, finishing all nine of his races to pick up nine finisher's medals.

'It used to make me laugh when people said I wasn't a real road racer just because I didn't race at the TT … I loved racing at Scarborough and you don't get more of a road circuit than Scarborough.'

BARRY SHEENE

'Some of the best races I've had have been after a good bedroom session.'

BARRY SHEENE

◄ Despite his crash in the 125cc Isle of Man TT race, Barry still took part in the Production race the following day on a borrowed 250cc Crooks Suzuki. He again posted good times in practice, but during the race he suffered a speed wobble, and the seat, petrol tank, steering damper and battery all worked their way loose. He pulled in after one lap — and never raced at the TT again.

▲ Barry on a Hi-Tac Suzuki T500 motorcycle in December 1971. The machine was the work of constructor Colin Seeley and Sheene rode it in 1972.

▶ The 1971 season saw Barry turn professional aged just 20. This meant that he could concentrate on his racing career – and travelling round the world and getting paid to race motorcycles was a far more attractive proposition than driving a lorry around Central London or giving out tickets as a car park attendant. His good looks, relatively young age and shoulder-length hair meant he stood out on the racing scene, and he was increasingly attracting the attention of fans and sponsors.

'The support of the fans is really nice, it makes everything worthwhile, but I don't think I'm anything special.'

BARRY SHEENE

▲ Barry enjoys a pre-race cigarette as he leaves the pits while legendary mechanic Nobby Clark (right) looks on. In 1972 Sheene signed to ride a works Yamaha YZ635 in the 250cc World Championship under French importer Sonauto's banner. At the beginning of the year, Barry was the hottest property in motorcycle racing, but a combination of complacency, loss of form and unreliable machinery meant this was a year to forget. He should have been challenging for the 250cc and 350cc World titles, but his only points all year were a third and a fourth on the 250 in two Grands Prix, Spain and Austria.

▶ 1972 was a season when nothing went right, but 1973 was a year that put Barry's career firmly back on track. It was the beginning of a seven-year period as a works Suzuki rider and in that first season Sheene targeted three titles – the FIM Formula 750 Championship and Britain's two most prestigious national championships, the MCN Superbike and ShellSport 500. Barry won the newly formed Formula 750 European Championship while his success in the 1973 Shellsport series can be seen by the number of stars adorning the side of his motorcycle. Winning riders were given one for every victory in the event.

'In 1973 the works Suzukis were feeling right; I was beginning to feel right; and I sensed there might be something good at last happening for me.'
BARRY SHEENE

◄ Barry was given two machines by Suzuki for 1973 — an air-cooled TR500 and a three-cylinder water-cooled TR750. Both bikes were developed from road bikes, but they were housed in frames built by chassis specialist and former sidecar champion Colin Seeley. The superior handling of the bikes, combined with Barry's own mechanical skills, ensured the partnership was a success: the Seeley-framed TR750 triple, seen here, gave Barry victory in both the FIM F750 Championship and MCN Superbike series.

◄ As Barry's career gained momentum, his earnings as a professional racer began to improve, and by the end of the 1972 season he had enough money to move out of London. He eventually settled on Ashwood Hall, a six-bedroom country farmhouse near Wisbech in Cambridgeshire. Although in need of renovation, it had its own grounds and an apple orchard, and – crucially for Barry – it was big enough to provide a home for both him and his parents, Franco and Iris.

▲ By his own admission, Barry put his parents through hell as a rebellious teenager. As he got older, though, his bond with them grew: not only were they always by his side at a race meeting, they also shared a home with him. So whenever Barry moved house, Franco and Iris always went with him. His dad's expertise with machinery has been well documented and he was vital in giving set-up advice throughout Barry's career, but equally important was his relationship with his mother. Their bond was incredibly tight right up until she passed away in June 1991, which left him distraught. So keenly did he feel her loss, sister Maggie felt it was 'something he never really got over'.

CHAPTER 2

THE RISE, FALL AND REMOUNT OF A CHAMPION

If I could rewind time, I wouldn't change anything. Well, apart from not running Dunlops at Daytona in 1975 and making sure they had enough bloody marshals at Silverstone in 1982.'

THE RISE, FALL AND REMOUNT OF A CHAMPION

It took around eight seconds, 300 yards of falling, one Thames TV film crew and broken bones in his thigh, arm and leg for Barry Sheene to make the journey from the track to the operating theatre to the nation's sofa. 'If I'd been a racehorse they would have shot me,' he later said.

His 175mph crash in March 1975 at Daytona was a disaster that could easily have been the end of a life and career. Instead, the horror show pricked at Britain's voyeurism and made him famous. The six-week fightback, achieved with what seemed to the public like charismatic ambivalence, and then his swift ascent to the top of the world, was a *Boy's Own* war story. Little wonder that Martyn Ogborne, his chief mechanic, recalled: 'I said to Barry, "If you'd been in the Second World War, you'd have been a bloody Spitfire pilot." I have never seen such determination. All we understood was we had to get Barry's machine here in England ready in six weeks or less! People just laughed.'

It seemed apposite that Barry's nadir should come in front of cameras, and the subsequent documentary was his

◀ Barry warms up the 500cc Heron Suzuki prior to a non-Championship 500cc race at Chimay in Belgium in June 1976, a last-minute cigarette part of his pre-race preparations. Such events were generating large crowds as the popularity of motorcycle racing increased. French jeans manufacturer Mashe were one of the first companies to pay to sponsor Sheene and have their logos emblazoned on his helmet and leathers.

platform to display his skill and personality. Rattling off his manifold injuries to a lens with the pay-off quip, 'Other than that, I feel brand new', he was a natural showman. Certainly, he attracted an audience and caught the attention of model Stephanie McLean, who would become his wife and confidante, an ever-present figure in the pits and paddocks of the world.

However, while his *News at Ten* crashes caused the nation to wince, the remarkable chronology is often forgotten. He made his self-imposed deadline to come back at Cadwell Park and found he could still ride even if he had a 46-centimetre (18-inch) rod in his thigh. For the first Grand Prix of the season, the team went to the notorious Salzburgring circuit in Austria, known colloquially as Tin Can Alley because the track was lined with metal barriers. However, in this era of push-starts, officious organisers refused to allow the handicapped rider to begin from the back of the grid with a designated pusher. If that was frustrating, the scale of the task and risk lying ahead was later made known to Ogborne. 'I asked a surgeon about racing with a metal pin in the thigh bone and he told me that if the bone broke again it would simply shatter. Barry had to teach himself to ride with that scenario in the back of his mind. He went into battle – and that is what it was then – knowing he could never afford to throw the machine away at any time.'

It was a horrible predicament that would hover over him for two long years, through the shattered knee he

'He went into battle knowing he could never afford to throw the machine away at any time.'

suffered after obliging fans by pulling a wheelie at the end of 1975 and all the way to the start of the 1977 season when a doctor finally removed the pin with a large hammer. Again, the cameras were there; carnage and catharsis were played out on the small screen, but his was a wide-screen drama of broad scope and fine margins.

Three months later, at his first post-crash Grand Prix in Assen, Holland, Barry won his maiden 500cc world championship race. He did it at a fabled old road circuit, known as the Cathedral of Motorcycling, and in some style, playing with the mind (it was cruel and just for the hell of it) of the most successful racer of them all, Giacomo Agostini, before finally passing him on the last lap.

Off the track, 1975 would be a crossroads too and his pursuit of women would end with Stephanie. However, the extracurricular frivolity remained unchecked into the 1990s with the formation of the Squadron, a ribald band of brothers with Barry as Wing Commander. One member recalled Barry not only escaping a parking ticket on the King's Road but also persuading the traffic warden 'to get her tits out, which he signed with a marker pen.

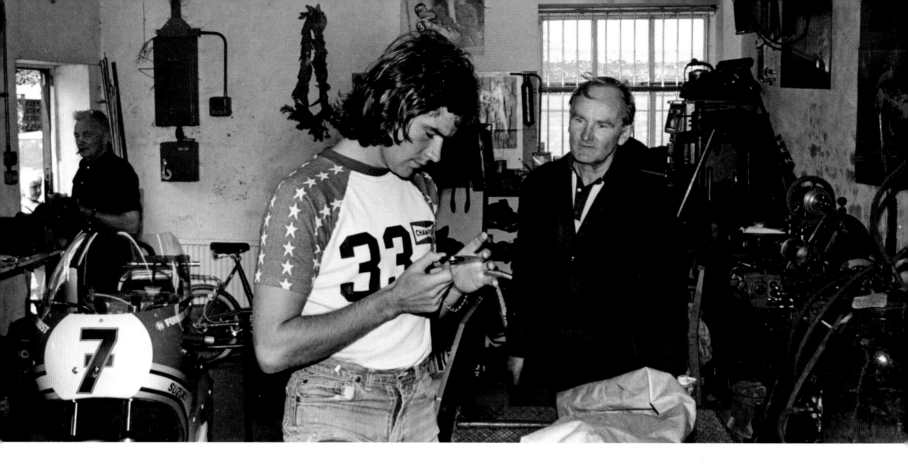

His fan base grew and Barry would spend hours signing autographs. Some of his working-class northern peers regarded him as a cocky southerner with a flash van. Flash he might have been, but he was determined that the sport could not continue as it was: unsafe, unwashed and unseen on the periphery.

The rivalries intensified in tandem with Barry's dominance in 1976. On his peerless Suzuki he won the first four races he entered, skipping the Isle of Man TT as it made its farewell bow as a World Championship round. The first racer to beat him that year was John Williams, a compatriot and fellow Suzuki rider, but a man whose gratitude was grudging when Barry probably saved his life ahead of the title-decider in Sweden. Seeing Williams

His everyman appeal meant he could party with lords and splash it on with Henry Cooper

fall in a practice session, Barry stopped and freed his tongue. Williams struggled to fully acknowledge the debt he owed Sheene all the way to his death in a road race two years later.

By then Phil Read, twice the World Champion and once a friend, had also become a sworn enemy following a row. Could Barry and should Barry have helped his compatriot in his 1975 title duel with Agostini?

Barry could not have cared less. He had won the world title with four rounds to spare and so didn't bother to turn up for the last races of the year. If some later suggested he didn't have a stellar field to test him in 1976, his dominance provided proof of his skill. That he did it all so soon after the trauma of Daytona was proof of a unique psyche.

By the start of the following season he was sitting at sport's top table, a friend of motorsport fan George Harrison and co-conspirator of Formula One hedonist James Hunt, but with an everyman appeal that meant he could party with lords and splash it on with Henry Cooper. Not that Stephanie would have approved of too much Brut 33. 'I'd have gone mad if he'd have splashed that all over him,' she told a documentary film crew. 'We had buckets of it, so we would give it to his uncle, who used to stink of it.'

The scent of success endured through 1977, though it was never easy, according to Ogborne, who recalled that, despite his injuries, his man had developed incredible upper-body strength and stamina. 'Every time we went to Venezuela he won. Now that was a true endurance test, not only at the circuit but even getting your machines out of the airport without being killed or arrested. If you were unlucky enough to crash, you were advised to stand up quickly, as the circuit was surrounded by rattlesnakes. It was 48°C in the shade, and riders and mechanics were passing out."

Barry ignored the ice that workers cut with machetes, after hearing it was contaminated, and instead sucked on the peel of a lime before expelling it during the race. Like most things that year, it worked.

Pat Hennen's Suzuki and the Yamahas of Steve Baker and Johnny Cecotto were no match. Rod now removed from his thigh, he was an explosive force. His power was such that an ultimatum he issued to the team saw a new manager, Rex White, brought in, and to the outside world it was business as usual: a year of relentless superiority marred only by more tragedies on the track and further safety issues.

Barry was a maverick, willing to mouth strong opinions, and he took such matters seriously. This was why he led the bulk of the field in a boycott at the Salzburgring that year, following a horrendous crash and the death of Hans Stadelmann. Some critics have suggested that Barry was

'… the circuit was surrounded by rattlesnakes. It was 48°C in the shade and riders and mechanics were passing out.'

in some way lacking bravery when it came to this most treacherous track. The argument is risible: the truth lay in his knowledge of the cost of living fast.

Yet the Isle of Man legacy followed him and fans at Oliver's Mount road circuit at Scarborough, loyal to Yorkshire hero Mick Grant, would even throw beer cans at him. Barry wondered whether it was his way of doing things that so irked the people he characterised as tattooed, brown ale drinkers. As for his bravery, if the comeback did not convince the casually sceptic, then his astonishing 137.149mph lap at Spa – the fastest ever recorded in a Grand Prix – should have done. Factor in the slow sections and Barry's average speed on such narrow roads strained credulity. Ogborne kept a grisly record of deaths in the Suzuki GB Race Team from 1969 to 1988; the final tally was 62. Barry was the quick and the brave.

In 1976 Britain had celebrated having world champions in both the 500cc and Formula One series, but James Hunt faded to fifth on four wheels in 1977, leaving Barry to fly the flag.

His sixth win of the season in Sweden took him to Finland and the edge of victory. Steve Baker needed to win to keep alive his gossamer hopes, but he struggled with mechanical gremlins. Barry's Suzuki was also plagued by an overheating problem and so he settled for the sixth place that he needed to clinch the crown.

His status was now undisputed and he could again afford to sit out the remaining rounds, only coming out for the British Grand Prix at the end of the season. It was a race that showed the precariousness and precociousness of his racing life. Having been forced to retire through bike failure, he stood on the pit wall and watched his great friend, Steve Parrish, head towards victory. Parrish had just one lap to go to win the first Silverstone Grand Prix and finish third in the world championship when he spotted his friend leaning over the wall and brandishing a board. Barry had scrawled in chalk, 'Gas it wanker'. Parrish obliged and crashed. It effectively cost him his seat alongside Barry for 1978.

Sporting success is fleeting, even when fame lingers, and Kenny Roberts changed things. The teak-tough, hard-nosed Californian soon arrived on the Grand Prix scene, redefining riding with his rear-end slides and dirt-tracking past. If Barry had not had a true arch-rival before, he now dragged the sport to centre stage with another all-time great.

They fought and bickered and initially exchanged wins, Barry's season opener in Venezuela followed by Kenny's in

Spain, but the world championship hat-trick attempt was undermined by a debilitating, strength-sapping virus. It festered for months, but Barry was still only three points adrift by the time of a British Grand Prix that descended into farce: rain, pit stops and confusion gave way to a shortened race and timekeepers cutting through the mayhem with the declaration that the American had won. The title went down to the wire, where Roberts became King Kenny with a 10-point margin.

The 1979 season would see Roberts continue his success on his Yamaha, while Barry's flat-lining relationship with Suzuki would end in acrimonious divorce at the end of the year, following a season of discontent and mechanical failures. The two protagonists joined forces to back the new World Series, an ill-fated attempt to wrest control

The Japanese winter provided excellent conditions for some high-speed testing. Barry and mechanic Ken Fletcher get to enjoy a breather and survey proceedings from higher ground.

from the much-loathed Fédération Internationale de Motocyclisme (FIM), and this year also featured the seminal 1979 British Grand Prix, a race of derring-do, passing moves and Barry's two-fingered salute. 'He's waving at Roberts,' Murray Walker said with a delicious euphemistic flourish. Barry refused to accept second best and so came within an inch of the edge of the track and 0.03 seconds of his rival after a move on the final turn. 'It might as well have been three laps,' he said, but it was testament to his authorship of great sporting chapters that nobody would forget his greatest defeat.

Barry won his last Grand Prix with Suzuki at Le Mans before riding Yamahas, but his time as a title-challenger was over. Yet the story ran and ran. There was another Grand Prix win in 1981 in Sweden – the last of 19 in the 500cc class and the last by a Briton for 35 years. He still

Kenny Roberts removed his rival's helmet and likened what he saw to a 'plane crash'.

had the class and courage. Freddie Spencer, the world champion in 1983 and 1985, remembers watching Barry at Silverstone in 1982 and 'just smiling' at his pace. World champion again was an easy assumption. 'A few minutes later it was over.' He fell at 165mph on a track where multiple classes were practising at the same time. Ogborne too thought that the championship should have been his, pointing out that Franco Uncini, the champion, failed to score any points in the final three races.

Speculation is redundant, though. Barry hit the stricken Yamaha of Patrick Igoa, a 250cc rider, as he shot over a blind summit. They ended up in neighbouring beds in hospital. This time there would be metal plates and 27 screws in Sheene's legs. Roberts, one of the first on the scene, removed his rival's helmet and likened what he saw to a 'plane crash'.

Barry came back again and was still making the podium in his last season in 1984, but he retired the following January. World titles bookended by two awful accidents summed up the highs and lows; the rise, fall and remount of an indomitable character. He was dubbed 'bionic', but he was also flesh and blood and broken bone. Britain has never had a sportsman like him.

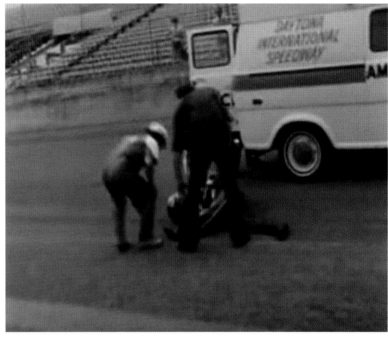

◀ The Daytona 200 in America was the traditional curtain-raiser to the international road-racing season, but the 1975 meeting was one that was going to change Barry's life forever. He had gone into the event as one of the pre-race favourites and his growing reputation meant that a television crew led by award-winning producer Frank Cvitanovich accompanied him to catch the build-up and race.

'I had just nicked sixth gear and the bike was not far short of 180mph, perhaps around 178mph,' said Barry. 'Suddenly it happened. The rear wheel locked solid. I immediately grabbed the clutch lever, but to no effect and the bike had a mind of its own. The sensation of the machine swinging sideways in a sudden jerking movement was terrifying. Together we went crazily down the banking and I was projected over the handlebars with maximum velocity.'

On 28 February 1975, Barry had completed five laps of his practice session and was hitting speeds of over 170smph around the banking when rubber from the rear wheel flew off and locked the rear wheel. Within an instant, the rear wheel came round and catapulted Barry over the handlebars and flung him over 100 yards down the road. Amazingly, he was still conscious, but he'd sustained a broken left femur, a right wrist, forearm, six ribs and collarbone. It was the fastest crash in motorcycle racing history, and Barry was suddenly on the front pages of newspapers and on television screens all around the world as millions of viewers witnessed the crash footage for themselves. Sheene became a national hero overnight.

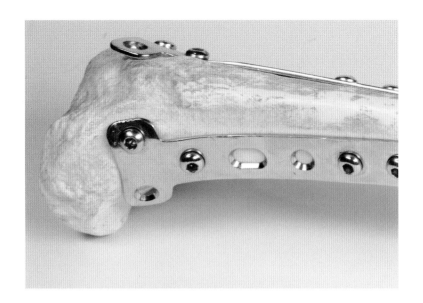

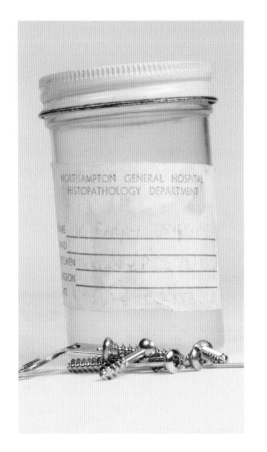

'Broken femur, collarbone and ribs, busted wrists and forearm, and a lot of skin off in the wrong places... Other than that, I feel brand new.'
BARRY SHEENE

▶ Although Barry was back racing within seven weeks of the Daytona crash, he suffered for some years afterwards, particularly with his circulation. Former Suzuki boss Maurice Knight sometimes witnessed Barry massaging his legs for up to 30 minutes in the morning before he could start his day. The 18-inch steel pin used to repair his thigh was removed under the watchful eye of a live television audience, the surgeon famously using a mallet to hammer the pin out of Barry's leg!

'… after the Daytona crash, I wasn't worried about whether I could race again.'
BARRY SHEENE

◄ A relaxed Barry returned to the saddle in late April 1975 for a national race meeting at Cadwell Park, just over seven weeks after the Daytona crash.

The Daytona crash ruled Sheene out of the first two rounds of the nine-round 1975 FIM Formula 750 series and two rounds of the 500cc World Championship. In the 750 series, a broken exhaust ended Sheene's race hopes at Mettet in Belgium and it was only at Magny Cours in France that he gained his first points and victory. Further victories came at Anderstorp in Sweden and at his home round at Silverstone. But just when it looked like he would regain the FIM Formula 750 series crown, he stepped off a trials bike at another meeting at Cadwell Park at 7mph, only for his injured right leg to give way and fold painfully beneath him. Sheene's season ended as it had started – in hospital – paving the way for Aussie Jack Findlay to take the title by a solitary point.

In the 500cc World Championship, Sheene was forced to miss the French and Austrian Grands Prix, but he recovered in time to take the chequered flag in the Dutch Grand Prix and Swedish Grand Prix. He came sixth in the final title standings with 30 championship points, the legendary Italian rider Giacomo Agostini a distant winner with 84 points. The Daytona crash had certainly handicapped Sheene, but nothing would hold him back in the 1976 World Championship …

The 1975 season was a defining moment for the careers of both Barry and Suzuki: this was the year the combination won their first 500cc Grand Prix.

◄ Barry continued to race the 750cc Suzuki and again contested the Formula 750 Championship in 1975, when he was again competitive. Wins were taken in France, Sweden and Great Britain, but he lost out to Jack Findlay in the title race, the Australian's consistency giving him a one-point advantage at season's end.

◄ A delighted Barry is driven on a lap of honour after winning the 1975 John Player Special International event at Silverstone. With the British Grand Prix still taking place on the Isle of Man, Silverstone hosted a major International race every year before finally, in 1977, becoming the venue for the British Grand Prix for the first time. The 1975 meeting comprised two legs, which counted towards the FIM Formula 750 series. Barry won both and he ended the year second overall, after taking maximum points at the three races he finished. Kawasaki's Barry Ditchburn (obscured) finished runner-up in the first leg.

'After I dismounted people seemed to be everywhere around me offering congratulations.'
BARRY SHEENE

▲ Barry may have been the rider, but it was very much a team effort that got him onto the top step of the podium. Dad Franco, girlfriend Stephanie and his army of mechanics all worked tirelessly to give their man the best chance of victory.

◄ Sheene started the 1976 World Championship season in the best way possible by winning the opening Grand Prix at Le Mans. He held off the talented Venezuelan Johnny Cecotto to win by nearly 4 seconds.

The Austrian circuit of Salzburgring was the venue for the second round of the 1976 500cc World Championship (shown here) and Barry claimed pole position by a second from Cecotto (3) on the factory Yamaha. The front row also featured Marco Lucchinelli (40), Phil Read (2), Tepi Lansivouri (4) and Michel Rougerie (20). Read led in the opening laps before Lansivouri took over. Sheene was very much in contention and re-took the lead with 13 laps to go. The Suzuki rider was never threatened again, eventually taking the win from Lucchinelli by almost 14 seconds.

▲ Barry gets some essential rest in between practice sessions at the 1976 Austrian Grand Prix.

▲ Barry puckers up to the camera as he strolls round the Salzburgring paddock for the 1976 Austrian Grand Prix. Traditionally held at the beginning of May each season, the circuit was surrounded by alpine forests. The paddock looks empty here, but by the time Friday arrived it was packed to the hilt – and the hillsides all the way round the 2.6-mile course were similarly crowded. The weather was always unpredictable – it could be freezing cold with rain or even snow, or the sun could be beating down.

◀ To add to his opening round victory in France, Barry's assault on the 1976 500cc World Championship continued in earnest at round two in Austria with a crushing 14-second victory over Marco Lucchinelli.

▲ The front row line-up at the start of the 1976 Italian 500cc Grand Prix at Mugello: Barry Sheene (7) waits for starters orders alongside Johnny Cecotto (55), Tepi Lansivouri (4), Phil Read (2) and Virginio Ferrari (28).

▶ The third round of the 1976 500cc World Championship took place at Mugello, Italy, and saw Barry tighten his grip on the title with his third successive victory. The all-conquering MV Agusta was a shadow of its former self and the two-stroke Suzukis and Yamahas would fight it out for the race wins, the former in particular. Barry was mounted on the official factory Suzuki entry, but old-stager Phil Read, already a seven-times world champion, had secured a privateer machine for the season and there was nothing between the two for the entire 29-lap race distance. On the run to the line on the final lap, Barry nosed ahead and got the verdict – albeit by just one-tenth of a second!

'I can't stand people who are legends in their own lunchtime.
I'm the sort of bloke who, if you've got time for me,
I've got time for you.' BARRY SHEENE

▲ The British round of the 1976 World Championship was once again held on the Isle of Man as part of the TT (albeit for the final time), so Barry opted out, resuming his challenge for the 500cc World Championship at Assen in Holland. He set pole position, but a poor start left him sitting on the line trying to coax the 4-cylinder 2-stroke Suzuki to fire cleanly, and he was mired in the pack. He set off 22nd out of a field of 27, but he was soon tearing through the pack, overhauling the likes of Karl Auer (8), Giacomo Agostini (1) and Phil Read (9), and was already up to eighth at the end of the opening lap. During practice, Barry had lapped the Dutch circuit two seconds quicker than anyone else and he crossed the finish line with hands raised after winning by a massive 45 seconds from American Pat Hennen.

▶ The Dutch Grand Prix at Assen was held in sweltering temperatures of almost 38°C on 27 June 1976. The race was the sixth round of the 500cc World Championship and gave Barry his fourth win of the series. His grip on the title strengthened as he moved on to 60 points, opening up an already formidable looking 38-point lead over the nearest challengers, Phil Read and Marco Lucchinelli.

◄ Barry was blessed with a huge amount of natural ability and switching back and forth between a wide range of bikes didn't cause him any problems. One of his biggest strenghths was his adatability and he never got engulfed in the 'red mist' that descended upon other riders. Indeed, 1970s photographer Vic Barnes described him as a master of improvisation, someone who analysed all around him and reacted accordingly, dropping one plan of attack and adopting another as the drama unfolded.

'I thought Barry was a cheeky little sod, very cocky and outrageous.'
STEPHANIE SHEENE

◀ Chimay in Belgium hosted one of the numerous non-Championship international races that were held during the 1976 season. These prestigious events attracted the sport's stars, offering substantial start and prize money. Chimay took place in June and so, when many riders were on the Isle of Man for the British Grand Prix, Barry headed to the 6.4-mile Belgium road circuit instead. There he duly won the 500cc race from Grand Prix rivals Phil Read and Marco Lucchinelli, who had also opted not to compete in the race held as part of the Isle of Man TT. He's pictured here with Lucchinelli (obscured, left) and his good friend the American Gary Nixon (right).

▶ Barry enjoys a loving embrace with his girlfriend, the model Stephanie McLean. The couple met after Stephanie saw Barry on TV and thought modelling his leathers would be a different idea and a good addition to her portfolio. With the duo both represented by IMG, she was able to contact him directly and the duo soon became inseparable, forming one of the most glamorous couples of the 1970s. Stephanie recalled about meeting him: 'I thought Barry was a cheeky little sod, very cocky and outrageous.'

Her appearance alongside Barry at the 1976 French Grand Prix became a press sensation and only added to the aura surrounding Sheene. Barry's life changed and Stephanie, like his parents, would be by Barry's side at all of his races from that moment on.

◀ The sight of Barry wearing a Gary Nixon t-shirt soon became familiar to everyone. Although he was wearing it when he crashed at Daytona, it was his lucky charm and he never raced without it.

▶ Barry cruising at Mallory Park in 1976. Barry's Texaco Heron Suzuki teammate for the 1976 World Championship season was John Williams. The pair were far from friends, Williams believing he should have been on equal machinery, but Barry was the dominant rider with Williams registering only one championship win at Spa-Francorchamps for the Belgium Grand Prix.

Barry's strongest opposition came from a number of other Suzuki riders, although they had the disadvantage of racing on the production version of the RG500. Phil Read ran him close in the opening rounds, before sensationally quitting Grand Prix racing midway through the season. Other significant threats came from Tepi Lansivouri, Pat Hennen, Marco Lucchinelli and the 15-times World Champion Giacomo Agostini. Suzuki ultimately filled 11 of the top 12 positions at the conclusion of the season.

'I remember in the old days, after I'd won the world title, I'd sit on the end of a lorry at some race meeting talking for an hour to a 10-year-old if he wanted to.'

BARRY SHEENE

◄Barry lifts the front wheel of the RG500 Suzuki as he crests the rise of Deer's Leap at Oulton Park in April during the 1976 season. He was contesting the 500cc World Championship, but competing in the domestic championships remained part of his contract with Suzuki and it was something Barry was keen to do in order to repay his loyal fans. The MCN Superbike and Shellsport 500cc Championships, as well as the Transatlantic Trophy races against the USA, were always contested where there was no clash with the Grand Prix calendar.

▲ In addition to the 500cc World Championship, Sheene continued to compete in the 1976 FIM Formula 750 series. He competed in six of the ten rounds, but Barry's 750 Suzuki-3 was dogged with reliability problems, meaning he secured just one point-scoring finish – third at Imola on 4 April. Barry is seen here chatting to Victor Palomo, and it was the Spaniard – an ex-water skiing World Champion – who ended up as champion. Despite failing to score at the first three rounds, a run of three victories at the end of the season saw him come out on top and have his finest moment on two wheels.

▶ As the most famous motorcycle racer in the world during the 1970s, Barry was more than used to being surrounded by his fans as they looked to get as close as possible to their hero.

'I was in no doubt I would win the title,
provided the bike did not strike trouble.
No one could tell me any different.' BARRY SHEENE

'I don't think there's many real friends to be had in racing. If you've got more than half a dozen, you have to ask yourself who the genuine ones are.'

BARRY SHEENE

◄ The Mallory Park circuit in Leicestershire played annual host to the International Race of the Year meeting, an end of season non-Championship event that regularly attracted the world's finest road racers along with crowds in excess of 50,000. Traditionally held in September, when the Grand Prix World Championships had ended, Barry won back-to-back races in 1974 and 1975. Here, in 1976, however, he had to settle for second behind American sensation Steve Baker. Alongside Barry on the grid is eight times World Champion Phil Read (2).

'I enjoyed every race I rode in 1976. It was so nice to clinch the world championship and it was something I'd set my heart on ever since I started racing. To finally achieve it made all the hard work and pain of crashing in '74 and '75 worthwhile.' BARRY SHEENE

◄ With the 1976 500cc World Championship won, Barry returned to the UK circuits as a hero. He didn't always come out on top, like the second place finish at the Mallory Park Race of the Year mentioned previously, but that mattered little to the British public. They idolised him whether he finished first, second or third. Wherever Barry raced, his fans flocked to see him displaying slogans and messages from the grandstands and grass banks, and surrounding him upon his return to the paddock.

► Barry never hid his love of cigarettes and nearly always enjoyed a crafty drag prior to the race. He gave up smoking in 1998.

Barry clinched his maiden 500cc World Championship at Anderstorp, Sweden on 25 July, 1976, in convincing fashion. It wasn't all plain sailing though as he was caught napping at the start and had to fight hard to come through the pack. Once there, the only man to challenge him was Tepi Lansivouri. The Finn's hopes were dashed when the swinging-arm fixing bolt came loose and he had to slacken the pace, eventually finishing fourth. That left Barry clear in the lead and he eventually won the race by 34 seconds from Jack Findlay. This was his fifth victory from six starts. He was finally world champion.

The scene afterwards, with Stephanie and Franco naturally among the first to congratulate him, was typically chaotic. Speaking to *Motor Cycle* after the race he could barely believe the magnitude of his achievement. 'I still don't know if it's true. It's hard to know how it feels at the moment and all I can say is that I want to thank the rest of the team for their help during the season.'

▲ When he returned to the UK for the end-of-season international meetings, his status as a national hero was confirmed and at the Powerbike International at Brands Hatch in October, where he was surrounded by his adoring fans, who joined him in the celebrations.

▲ Barry became good friends with Gary Nixon on his first racing trip to America in 1971 and it was a friendship that continued right up until Barry's death; indeed, the two had weekly telephone conversations. Barry helped get Nixon a test with the factory Suzuki team in 1974 and when his friend was seriously injured it sat heavily on Barry's shoulders. His own accidents never led him to contemplate retirement, but the crash and injuries received by Nixon upset Barry greatly, and he later admitted that if his good buddy hadn't pulled through he might well have walked away from the sport.

▶ Barry's team may have been small but it was close knit with dad Franco beside him throughout. He also had a group of loyal mechanics during his career including Don Mackay, Martyn Ogborne and Ken Fletcher and it was a highly successful team. They got the best out of the RG500 Suzuki with Barry's technical and mechanical skills playing a huge part not only in the set-up, but also in securing every possible gain over his rivals.

'My best moments were the fun times off the circuit and mucking about in the paddock.' BARRY SHEENE

'The 500cc title is not just a garland of honour, it is a supreme test of nerve, skill, fitness and bloody-minded determination.'

BARRY SHEENE

◄ The 1977 season saw Barry continue with Suzuki for the fifth consecutive year. Despite being world champion, he continued to use his famous No.7 instead of taking the No.1 plate. Yamaha's hopes were pinned on Steve Baker and Johnny Cecotto, while Pat Hennen and Steve Parrish joined Barry at Texaco Heron Suzuki. Early indications suggested that it would be harder for Barry to win the title than it had been the year before because there was increased competition on the 1977 grid.

◄ For some riders, the start line was a nerve wracking place – but not for Barry. He was always a picture of relaxation moments before a race, often using it to his advantage as he looked to out-psyche his rivals. This is Barry on the starting grid prior to competing for Suzuki in a Superbike race at Brands Hatch, England, in 1977.

Barry had two competitive teammates at Texaco Heron Suzuki in 1977, Pat Hennen and Steve Parrish, but his biggest threat came from Yamaha and American ace Steve Baker. Baker and Hennen had already impressed in the UK during the Transatlantic Trophy match races, and it seemed that Barry would find it hard to retain the title.

However, while the duo did finish second and third overall, it was Barry who again ended the year as world champion with six wins being taken in Venezuela, Germany, Italy, France, Belgium and Sweden. Sixth place in Finland in August saw him clinch his second successive World Championship and at the conclusion of the 11-rounds, he was 27 points clear of runner-up Baker.

▲ The Spa-Francorchamps circuit in Belgium hosted the seventh round of the 1977 500cc World Championship and a brilliant start saw Barry take an early lead, but it was no start-to-finish romp to victory as Frenchman Michel Rougerie pushed him all the way.

The 10-lap 1977 Belgian Grand Prix at Spa saw Barry, Rougerie, Steve Parrish, Pat Hennen and Tepi Lansivouri battle each other in the early stages before Barry and Rougerie pulled away. Both repeatedly broke the lap record, Barry eventually claiming it at a staggering 137.149mph (the fastest lap ever recorded in a Grand Prix race), but Rougerie's superb ride ended on the penultimate lap when the piston broke on his RG500 Suzuki and he was forced to retire. Barry swept to his fifth win of the season to take another giant step towards retaining his 500cc world title.

▲ Barry's second race win of the 1977 season came at Hockenheim in Germany and it was another clear-cut victory. After taking pole position by over a second, he set a new lap record in the race on his way to a commanding nine second victory over team-mate Pat Hennen.

▲ Barry and the RG500 Suzuki were a hard act to beat and another key component of what was a formidable combination were the Michelin tyres. The French company worked tirelessly with Barry and were rewarded with two successive world championships.

▶ The 1977 500cc World Championship was perhaps more hard fought for Barry than his maiden title in 1976 but, at the same time, it was perhaps more impressive. The FIM changed the rules by allowing points from all 11 rounds count, instead of the best six, as in 1976, to make Barry, more than anyone else, contest all the rounds. The competition was more intense this time around, but it only took him one more race to clinch the title. Some critics pointed to his publicity machine as detracting from other British riders, but his success did the sport more good than harm.

For the first time since 1949, the British round of the World Championship moved to the mainland and Silverstone for 1977. This was the result of an increasingly large number of riders choosing to boycott the Isle of Man TT over safety concerns. Barry was one of the ringleaders, and throughout his career he was always ready to lead from the front and stand up for riders' interests.

Barry lined up on the grid for the 1977 British Grand Prix on pole position after beating Johnny Cecotto (Yamaha) by over half a second. The race, the final round of the season, turned out to be a damp and dismal affair though, and the anticipated battle between the two failed to materialise: Barry retired on the ninth lap of 28 with a blown head gasket and Cecotto followed not long after. Barry's mood then worsened as steam from the blown gasket misted his visor and he crashed into the pit wall! Only four riders completed the full 28 laps with victory going to Barry's team-mate Pat Hennen.

▲ Getting around the paddock in quick fashion was never a problem for Barry and Stephanie, with Suzuki again providing speedy transportation. Barry's shoulder-length hair, casual style of dress and boyish looks saw him become motorcycling's first pin-up. Photo shoots became the norm and not just for racing purposes; he became a regular in the tabloid newspapers and mainstream magazines too. Modelling, fan clubs and business ventures upset a few of the diehard fans, but he made motorcycling cool and fans all across the world took him to their heart.

▶ Health and safety was less of a concern in 1977 as Barry rides his bike around the paddock in just a t-shirt and no helmet. The paddock was often a chaotic place and open not just to mechanics, but also the media and fans in the days and hours prior to the racing.

▶ The 1978 season gave Barry an increased challenge from Heron Suzuki team-mate Pat Hennen. The accomplished dirt-track racer from Phoenix, Arizona, had become the first American to win a world championship race when he triumphed in Finland in 1976, and had finished third overall in both 1976 and 1977. He was immediately on the pace in 1978 too. The duo now contested the MCN/Brut 33 Superbike and Shellsport 500cc Championships and Hennen soon proved he hadn't joined the team to play second fiddle to Barry. Indeed, the pair never saw eye to eye.

Victory in the opening rounds of the Shellsport 500cc series gave the 24-year-old Texan an early championship lead and it wasn't until round three that Barry took his first win. After two defeats – he'd finished second in the first round before retiring in the second – victory at Oulton Park was both timely and morale-boosting. However, Hennen fought back straightaway at round five at Cadwell Park, passing Barry on lap three, raising the outright lap record and winning by a considerable margin. After five rounds, the score stood at 4–1 in the American's favour with 72 points to Hennen and 51 for Barry.

By June, Hennen was also lying in second place to fellow American Kenny Roberts in the World Championship, and he now headed to the Isle of Man TT, where he was making his second appearance. He smashed the outright lap record, becoming the first rider to lap the 37.73-mile Mountain Course in less than 20 minutes as he strove to win the Senior race, but he crashed heavily on the final lap, sustaining serious head injuries. He eventually recovered, but was never able to race again.

▶ The calm before the storm: Barry sits patiently on the Suzuki just before the beginning of a 500cc Grand Prix in 1978. As can be seen in the background, the grid was a very busy place in the 1970s and safety standards were often minimal both on the grid and trackside, where obstacles were plenty. Mechanics, sponsors, marshals, photographers and general fans would all be milling around on the grid just as a rider was trying to prepare himself for what lay ahead. Here, though, Barry seems very content and relaxed, firmly focused on the job in hand.

With two back-to-back 500cc world championships in 1976 and 1977, Barry found that the winter months brought him into the public eye more than ever. In January 1978 he became the latest subject of the popular *This is Your Life* TV series. Surprised and slightly bashful (although he later admitted Gary Nixon had tipped him off about it happening), Barry was the latest 'victim' of host Eamonn Andrews and his famous red book at the Horticultural Halls at the Sporting Motorcycle Show in London. For the 30-minute show, more than 19 million viewers tuned in.

Barry was awarded the MBE for services to motorcycling in the 1978 New Year's Honours list and shows off his award alongside dad Franco and mum Iris. Only two guests were allowed to accompany him to Buckingham Palace, and wife Stephanie insisted that he took his parents – and wore a suit. For once, Barry did as he was told!

'Now you be careful, young man.'
HRH QUEEN ELIZABETH WHEN PRESENTING BARRY WITH HIS MBE IN 1978

'Kenny Roberts couldn't develop a cold never mind a motorcycle.'
BARRY SHEENE

▶ With no other riders in sight, Barry leads Kenny Roberts through the iconic Eau Rouge during the 1978 500cc Belgium Grand Prix at Spa-Francorchamps. They were only battling for second, however, as Wil Hartog led the race – although team orders dictated he wait for Barry and let him by in order to reduce Roberts' then 12-point lead. However, on the penultimate lap, Suzuki gave the Dutchman the signal to go and win the race. Roberts then chose his moment to overtake and Barry, furious with Hartog for taking points off him, could only finish third.

Barry was 1.78 m (5'10") but had a 90-cm (36-inch) inside leg – this was a handicap on the smaller bikes, but an advantage on the bigger bikes. On the 500, he had his weight hard up against the fuel tank, which allowed the rear tyre to move around and forced the front tyre to 'bite' into the tarmac. As the tyres developed, his long legs acted as a third wheel.

◄ After two years of dominating the 500cc World Championship, Barry lost the title in the 1978 season to Kenny Roberts by ten points, the American winning by 110 points to Sheene's 100. Sheene had faced all manner of challenges, first from team-mate Pat Hennen and then from Roberts, who went on to win the title three years in a row between 1978 and 1980. Barry had also battled illness: after winning the opening race of the season in Venezuela in March, he started to feel unwell on the journey home and the illness refused to go away, playing a significant part in his early season performances. A viral infection was later revealed to be Bornholm disease, but he battled on, and as the season progressed, he recovered to be close to his best. It wasn't enough, though, and he lost his title.

◄ For the 1979 season, Barry had two new team-mates at Heron Suzuki: Ulsterman Tom Herron and Steve Parrish joined him to attack the 500cc World Championship and MCN Superbike and Shellsport 500cc titles. Parrish, a close friend of Barry, had previously ridden for the team in 1977. Herron was an expert on road circuits like the Isle of Man TT and North West 200, and had earned his ride after impressing in the 250cc and 350cc World Championships in the previous two seasons.

Two new versions of the RG500 were launched in 1979 and these were made available to all of the Suzuki-sponsored teams, including Heron Suzuki, Team Gallina and Team Nimag. Of the two versions, Barry preferred the one with the radiator placed in the nose of the bike, because it gave better handling, but Virginio Ferrari (Team Gallina) and Wil Hartog (Team Nimag) preferred the other. Outvoted two to one, Barry had to race the entire season on a machine he ultimately didn't like. It was clear Barry was no longer Suzuki's favourite son.

'After three or four Grands Prix on the trot it used to be great to get back to England, because I had such great support ... without those people you are nothing.'
BARRY SHEENE

▶ The UK team was humiliated by the USA in the 1979 Transatlantic Trophy races, losing by some 93 points. Seen here with fellow Brits Mick Grant (10) and Keith Huewen (16), Barry took three wins and a second in the first four races, but a sick engine and then a broken main bearing in the final two races at Oulton Park brought his hopes of captaining the UK to another victory to an end.

▲ Barry's victory in the 1977 500cc World Championship saw him get the better of his Yamaha rival Steve Baker by 27 points. By 1979, the American rider was back in the privateer ranks, but continued to enjoy close battles with Barry – none more so than in the annual Transatlantic Trophy Match Races. Pictured here at Brands Hatch in April that year, Barry won both races at the Kent venue in front of some 50,000 fans and millions more watching on TV. Baker struggled with an ailing Yamaha and an injured arm broken the previous year, and he managed just a 14th place.

Intent on proving the loss of his 500cc World Championship crown in 1978 was a mere blip, Barry set about making the 1979 title his. He got off to the best start possible, winning the opening round of the 1979 500cc World Championship in Venezuela. However, he then suffered disappointment at rounds two and three in Austria and Germany. Brake problems saw him finish

a disastrous 12th in Austria, and at Hockenheim a shattered big end bearing led to a 14th lap retirement. The situation was far from helped by the fact that his arch rival Kenny Roberts would go on to triumph in the German Grand Prix. With the season only three races old (and with 10 left to race), Sheene was already facing an uphill battle to regain his title.

Try as he might, Sheene continued to struggle to find top form, and over the next five races he recorded a fourth in Italy and second in Holland, failing to score in Spain, Yugoslavia and Belgium. By contrast, Roberts was victorious in three of the races. The season did see Sheene take the chequered flag in the Swedish and French Grands Prix, but it wasn't enough and, come the end of the season, Sheene finished third on 87 points (with three wins). He was 26 points behind Roberts, who had registered five Grand Prix wins that season, including the British Grand Prix.

▲ Powering along the Cooper Straight at Brands Hatch, the 1979 Transatlantic Trophy Match races saw Barry dominate proceedings with two race wins, although the British team was hammered in the overall points by the American underdogs.

▲ They may have been arch rivals, but Barry and Kenny Roberts had the utmost respect for each other and could still hang out in the race paddocks where the banter and jibes would, more often than not, be in frequent supply!

▶ Barry had countless battles with American ace Roberts, dating as far back as 1974, but the biggest, and most famous, of them all was the British Grand Prix at Silverstone on 12 August, 1979. Many consider the race to be one of the greatest Grands Prix of all time, Barry overcoming the speed advantage of Roberts' Yamaha with some brilliant overtaking manoeuvres on the brakes. The lead changed hands on numerous occasions, but the verdict ultimately went the way of Roberts by just 0.03 seconds. It was the closest Barry ever got to a British Grand Prix victory.

▲ Despite taking place over 30 years ago, the 1979 500cc British Grand Prix at Silverstone is still regarded as one of the greatest races ever and all three men on the podium – Barry, Kenny Roberts and Wil Hartog – played their part.

The trio soon broke away from the rest of the field and although Hartog slipped off the pace slightly at mid-race distance, Sheene and Roberts continued to battle for the lead. They continued to swap the lead throughout the 28-lap event, with Roberts winning ahead of Barry by the tiny margin of just 0.03 of a second.

'I really like the publicity – in the end it can only be good for motorcycling.' BARRY SHEENE

▶ 15-times World Champion Giacomo Agostini's career was coming to an end just as Barry's was reaching its peak — indeed, the Italian retired at the end of the 1977 season — but he remained a fixture in the paddock and his friendship with Barry continued. The Italian was known to enjoy the finer things in life and such was his admiration for Barry that he flew all the way from Italy to be part of the celebrations when Barry appeared on *This is Your Life*. Barry could be heard saying 'the party's going to start now' when Ago walked in and you can bet it didn't end until the small hours!

The mechanical skills Barry had gained as a child meant that he was very much 'hands on'. He was able to give in-depth feedback to his long-serving mechanics Don Mackay and Ken Fletcher after each practice session, which enabled them to find the best possible set-up.

▼ Barry takes on some pre-race fluids, essential when racing in temperatures that could exceed 38°C.

◄ Barry may have been chasing World Championship glory, but he was equally determined to sweep all before him whenever he raced – not just the domestic championships, in the form of the MCN Superbike and Shellsport 500cc series, but also the numerous non-championship internationals. 1979 was typically busy, and September's AGV Nations Cup meeting at Donington Park saw him take no less than four race wins against a star-studded field that featured the likes of Kenny Roberts, Wil Hartog, Gregg Hansford, Marco Lucchinelli and Graeme Crosby. He finished the season by winning the Powerbike International race at Brands Hatch to once again confirm that he was the UK's leading bike rider.

▲ After failing to win the 1979 500cc World Championship, Barry returned to the UK to contest the end-of-season Internationals and as well as being victorious at Donington Park and Brands Hatch, he dominated proceedings at the Gold Cup meeting at Oliver's Mount, Scarborough in September. Riding his 500cc Grand Prix machine, Barry won the prestigious Gold Cup for the third time in his career before switching to the larger capacity 680cc Heron Suzuki for the two 10-lap Duckhams/MCN Superbike Championship races. He claimed victory in both races, beating regular British rivals Dave Potter, Mick Grant and Roger Marshall, also setting a new outright lap record around the tricky 2.43-mile road circuit.

▲ Barry's biggest fear when it came to crashing was amputation and he simply couldn't bear the thought of losing a part of his body. For that reason, he rated his crash at the French Grand Prix at Paul Ricard on 25 May, 1980, as the worst of his career, despite the tally of injuries being far less than those he sustained at Daytona in 1975 and Silverstone in 1982.

Experiencing patter from the front end of the machine, Barry touched the front brake — and down he went. When the bike hit the tarmac, the little finger on his left hand was trapped under the right handlebar. Although he was otherwise unhurt, the damage to the finger was considerable. Surgeons in Marseille saved the finger with some fine surgery and wire, but when he made his return to racing, the finger was far from healed and was proving more and more troublesome. After three more operations to try to save it, he reluctantly agreed to have the top half of it amputated in July.

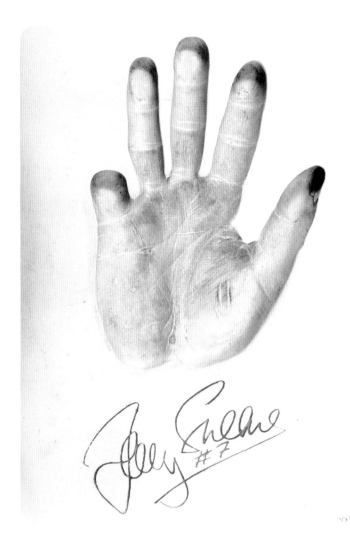

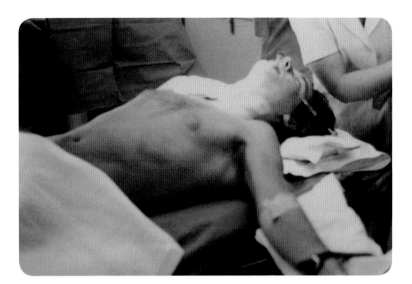

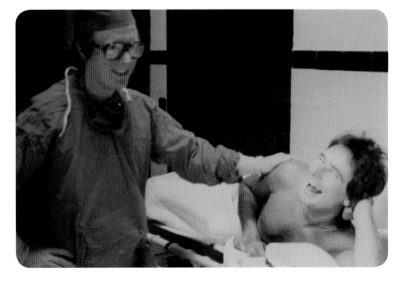

▲ A cast of Barry's hand showing the amputated little finger on his left hand, the result of the injury he sustained at the French Grand Prix in 1980.

▶ Barry had gone under the knife earlier that year, in March, when he had had a plate removed from his collarbone, the legacy of a crash earlier in his career in Belgium, when he broke the offending bone.

Sheene switched from Suzuki to Yamaha for the 1980 500cc World Championship season, but it soon became clear that Barry's privateer TZ500 Yamaha was no match for the works machines of Kenny Roberts and Johnny Cecotto or the Suzukis of Randy Mamola and Marco Lucchinelli. The first two rounds yielded only 10 points – fifth in Italy and seventh in Spain – and at the third round at the Paul Ricard circuit in France, Barry again had to ride over the limit just to try and stay in touch. On this occasion he tried too hard and was spat off the Yamaha while running in sixth.

Dad Franco and mechanic Ken Fletcher looked after both the 500cc and 750cc Yamahas during the season, but 1980, Barry's 10th year of Grand Prix racing, saw him go back to privateer status and as a result the season was hard.

◄ The 1980 season may have been difficult for Barry on the Grand Prix trail, but his decision to focus on the International meetings in Britain for the final third of the season proved wise – particularly at Oliver's Mount, Scarborough. Barry is seen here on his 750cc Akai Yamaha – on the approach to Mere hairpin and also when leaving the holding area. The feature Gold Cup eluded him on this occasion, but he took overall victory in the MCN Superbike Championship. Sharing first and second place finishes with Dave Potter, Barry equalled his own year-old lap record for a haul of 32 points, which moved him up to sixth overall in the title table, despite only contesting two rounds.

▲ After a hugely disappointing year in 1980, Barry knew that if he was to have any chance of fighting for the 500cc world title he'd need better machinery. Mitsui, Yamaha's British importers, agreed and they worked tirelessly to get him back in favour with the company in Japan. They secured Barry an invitation for a Yamaha-only event in Sugo at the end of the 1980 season and, although he crashed out of the second race while leading, he impressed Yamaha's management with his courage and determination. He was still not on the same spec machinery as Kenny Roberts, but he was rewarded with the promise of works machinery for the 1981 season and ace tuner Erv Kanemoto being added to his team.

Barry lined up alongside Roberts and other leading riders, including Randy Mamola and Graeme Crosby, at April's John Player Gold Cup meeting at Donington Park held on 11–12 April, 1981. The race saw Barry finish third on his across-the-frame four-cylinder Yamaha behind the two superior Suzuki bikes.

◀ He may not have been riding the strongest machine, but by the time Sheene arrived for the ninth race of the season – the British Grand Prix at Silverstone on 2 August – he was lying in fourth place in the 500cc World Championship. This was thanks to podium finishes in Italy and San Marino, and he was 31 points adrift of the championship leader Marco Lucchinelli. In addition, Sheene was given a new square-four-cylinder Yamaha at Silverstone and hoped that this would help him make a late challenge for the championship title.

It wasn't to be, though, and Sheene was again denied a maiden win at his home Grand Prix when Crosby crashed, taking both Barry and Lucchinelli down with him.

The Salzburgring circuit in Austria got the 1981 500cc World Championship season underway and it was the first opportunity for Barry to test both himself and the new Yamaha against all his Grand Prix rivals. The Suzuki riders Randy Mamola, Graeme Crosby and Hiroyuki Kawasaki dominated the race, and mechanic Ken Fletcher relayed the information to Barry during the race, his pit board here telling him he's in fourth position with three laps to go. That was where he finished, being the first Yamaha rider to take the chequered flag, and getting his world title campaign up and running in solid fashion.

▲ Barry preparing for a practice session in 1981.

▶ Barry takes the outside line on his 750cc Yamaha as Kork Ballington opts for the inside at the Mallory Park hairpin. Contesting the 1981 Race of the Year meeting, Barry eventually got the better of the South African rider, who finished third, but he had to settle for second at the end of the 40 laps, victory going to Kiwi Graeme Crosby. With development and production of the 750cc Yamaha coming to an end, it was rapidly becoming outgunned by the smaller, yet more nimble, 500cc machines and results were harder to come by. Barry did, however, win the prestigious race in 1974, 1975 and 1978.

Sheene bounced back from the Silverstone disappointment by winning the final round of the series at Anderstorp in Sweden on 16 August. This was his first Grand Prix victory since Le Mans, France, in September 1979.

He ended the 1981 500cc World Championship in fourth overall with 72 points, behind Randy Mamola and Kenny Roberts, and 33 points behind the championship winner Marco Lucchinelli.

At the end of the season, Barry was invited by Yamaha to Sugo, Japan, to take part in a number of test sessions in preparation for the following year. Victory at the Swedish Grand Prix, as well as his triumphs in prestigious end-of-season meetings in Spain and Malaysia, encouraged the Yamaha team bosses and helped improve Sheene's standing within Yamaha. Here he is enjoying a series of closed-season sessions testing machinery at Sugo, Japan, where he was promised superior machinery for the 1982 season.

▲ In 1982, with tobacco company John Player now the title sponsor of Barry's team, Yamaha provided him with a new, updated version of the 500cc square four called the OW60. He took rostrum finishes in Argentina, Austria, Spain, Holland, Belgium and Yugoslavia, but his hopes of receiving identical machinery to Kenny Roberts were shattered as early as the second round in Austria. There Yamaha wheeled out the V4 OW61 for the American. It was soon clear to Barry that his OW60 was down on power to the V4, but Yamaha had promised that he'd get the new model for his home Grand Prix at Silverstone. The OW61 was finally delivered to Barry on the Monday of race week and he needed only a few laps to realise that major changes were needed to the frame geometry.

▶ The changes were duly made and he got the bike back in time for unofficial practice on Wednesday, when his lap times were impressive. However, just after 4.30 p.m. on 28 July, Barry swept round Abbey Curve and ploughed into the wreckage of a 250cc Yamaha that had been in a collision with a 125cc MBA moments earlier. Barry hit the stricken machine at over 160mph, smashing the front end off the V4, and was catapulted into and over the handlebars. Launched some 10 metres into the air, Barry landed over 100 metres further down the track, unmoving and unconscious. The bike was torn and twisted into numerous lumps of metal.

'I came over the crest of the rise on my usual line and there was a bike lying in the road and I hit it. Then all I can recall seeing was a big ball of flame. Nothing else.' BARRY SHEENE

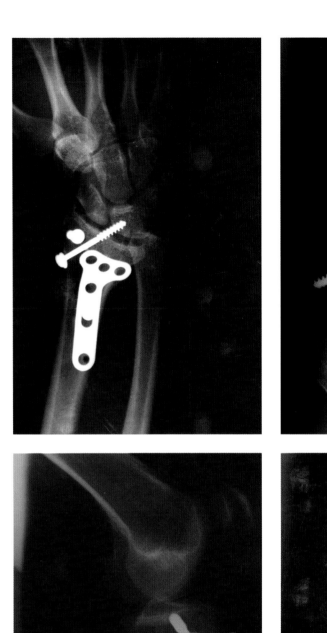
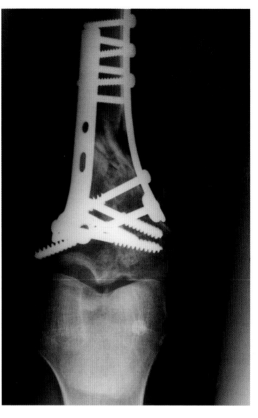
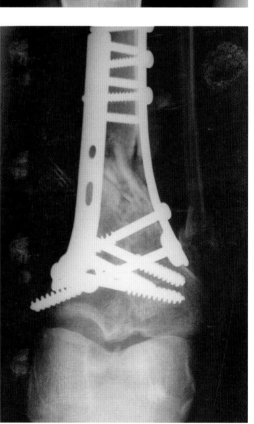
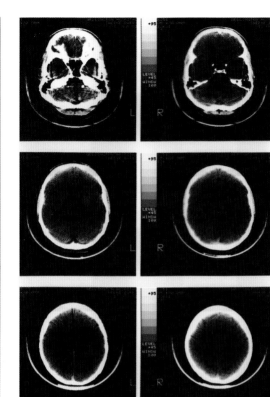
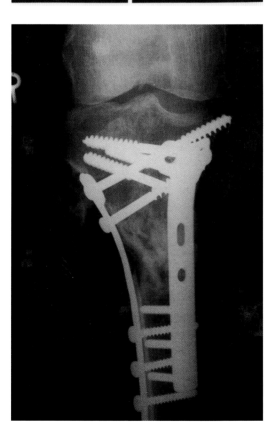

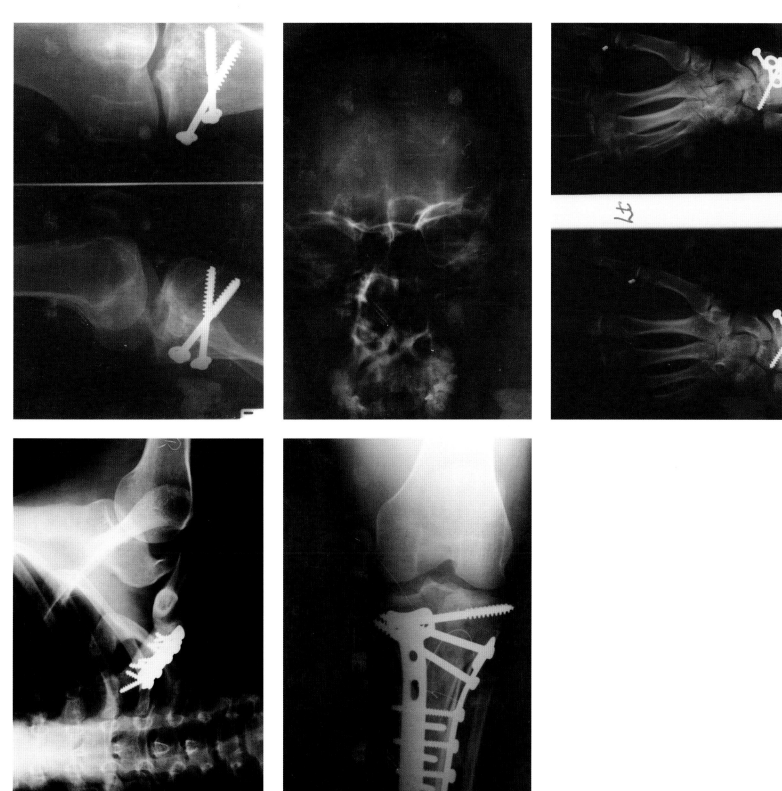

The x-rays from Barry's crash were shown on every news channel and printed in every newspaper, and astonished the general public: Barry was labelled the 'bionic man'.

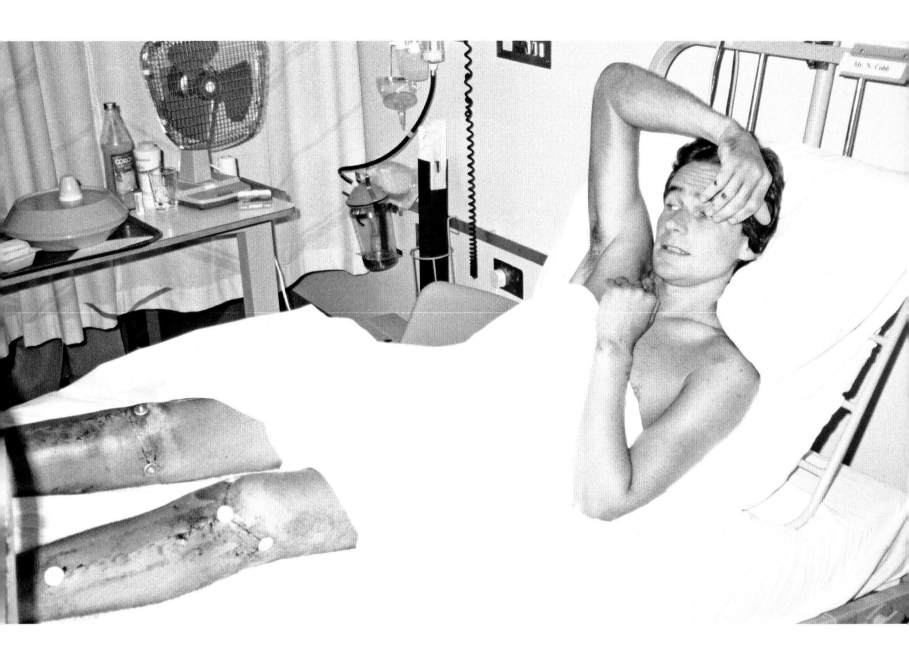

▲ Sheene was given regular doses of pethidine to numb the pain and, just like his response after the Daytona crash of 1975, his levels of recovery astounded everyone, particularly surgeon Nigel Cobb. The stitches that sewed his legs back together can be clearly seen here, and while Cobb usually discharged his patients after three months, Barry was discharged after just three and half weeks.

'I didn't consider myself as brave. All I had to do was get my legs mended as quickly as possible and get back on a bike.' BARRY SHEENE

▲ Barry knew that he was in for another long and painful road back to full fitness, but his high pain threshold and previous experiences meant he knew all about self-physiotherapy. His spirits remained high and he was back on a bike 10 weeks after the second crash of his career, which had almost claimed his life. With good friend Steve Parrish offering support, should anything go wrong, Barry completed two laps of Donington Park on this road-going RD350 Yamaha, the 25,000-strong crowd cheering him every inch of the way.

◀ When it came to Barry, nothing could surprise people. If anything came close, it was his decision while convalescing from his Silverstone crash to return to Suzuki for the 1983 season. Despite working his way back into favour with Yamaha and rewarding them with some fine results, Barry was irritated that he was never given machinery equal to that of Kenny Roberts, as he explained in his column for *Motor Cycle Weekly*. 'To be perfectly honest, I'm not sad to be leaving Yamaha. I was always promised the same machines as Kenny but never actually got them. The bikes were always designed to suit Kenny's style, which meant they were totally wrong for everyone else.'

However, when he returned to Suzuki he was once again at the foot of the ladder. With the factory bikes already having been given to Randy Mamola and Virginio Ferrari, all he had for 1983 were production RG500 machines. He was in playful mood with the photographer on this test day (left) and was spraying the champagne after the Transatlantic Trophy races, where the GB team, again captained by Barry, beat the USA by 245 points to 198. For Barry, though, it would prove to be a long and difficult year, scoring just nine points during the 500cc Grand Prix season.

'I've got more chance of being punched in the face by the Pope than finishing in the top three.'

BARRY SHEENE

◄ Coming back to Suzuki in 1983 after three years at Yamaha was the sort of challenge Barry relished, especially after the setback of the Silverstone crash the year before. Suzuki gave him two production versions of the RG500 and his first laps on them came at a snowy Donington Park in February. He got more laps on the bikes during March before heading off to Kyalami in South Africa for the opening round of the World Championship, a circuit he had last raced in 1972. Still confident in his own ability, the bikes were far from competitive, Barry stating: 'I have no chance of getting in the top six unless it rains.' Seventh in the French Grand Prix, at Le Mans on 2 April 1983, was his best result of the year, although ninth at Silverstone for the British Grand Prix on 31 July, 1983 saw him get the biggest cheer of the day from his ever faithful fans.

▲ Barry's outings on four-stroke machinery were most unusual. This rare picture, taken at Oulton Park in April 1983, shows Barry on the 997cc F1 Suzuki usually campaigned by team-mate Rob McElnea. When the four-stroke rider crashed and was injured in practice, Barry stepped in to try and help the Heron Suzuki team. Jumping on an unfamiliar bike at the last minute is always a tall order and he finished in a solid seventh place.

▶ Some of Barry's first race outings in 1983 came in the annual Transatlantic Trophy races, which kicked off at Oulton Park on Good Friday. He was given a year-old works RG500 Suzuki as the team looked to upgrade his machinery. Grand Prix rivals Kenny Roberts and Randy Mamola were in attendance on full factory spec machinery, and although Great Britain won comfortably, Barry could only manage a best finish of fourth from the six races held at Oulton (Friday, 30 April), Snetterton (Sunday, 1 May) and Brands Hatch (Monday, 2 May). He is pictured here riding past the parked cars, caravans and fans littered around the Oulton Park paddock.

'I always used to be in that [winning] position and I can still ride a bike … but to carry on racing I must have a faster bike.'

BARRY SHEENE

◀ Barry's return to Suzuki didn't yield the results he'd hoped for and the promise of better machinery failed to materialise. The whole season was a struggle with his best Grand Prix finish being a lowly seventh. This is Barry in reflective mood after a disappointing result at the Italian Grand Prix in 1983.

'I'd always planned to retire at 35 and had done everything I wanted to do. I was totally happy with myself – I was fulfilled, I had no regrets.'

BARRY SHEENE

◀ During the 1984 season it was becoming clear to Sheene that he was in the twilight of his motorcycling career. His last UK race win came on Sunday, 16 September at the Scarborough Gold Cup and Barry's final competitive outing came in the televised World of Sport Superbike race at Donington Park a week later on Saturday, 22 September. There was to be no fairy-tale victory, but he pushed eventual winner Ron Haslam all the way and only a photo finish could determine who had won. He admitted it had been fun and had felt like old times, and he didn't announce his retirement immediately since he was still working on a possible deal with Italian manufacturer Cagiva for 1985.

'I was riding as good as I'd ever done, but I got fed up with all the Japanese factory bullshit. If Cagiva had got their act together, I would have ridden for them in 1985, but they didn't and that was that. I'd always planned to retire at 35 and had done everything I wanted to do. I was totally happy with myself – I was fulfilled, I had no regrets.'

'There are other things in life besides motorcycle racing and you cannot do it for ever.'

BARRY SHEENE

◄ With his torn leathers behind him, a permanent reminder of his Daytona crash in 1975, Barry retired at the end of the 1984 season after a 17-year career. It was one he could look back at and reflect upon with pride. Two 500cc World Championships, 21 Grand Prix wins, a 750cc FIM European Championship title, five MCN Superbike Championships, five 500cc Shellsport Championships, two 125cc British Championships, five times winner of the MCN Man of the Year and an MBE awarded by the Queen – it's fair to say he'd achieved plenty.

▲ Barry's final win before retiring came at the International Gold Cup meeting at Oliver's Mount, Scarborough. He had made his debut at the circuit almost 15 years earlier and his love for the venue never waned: he was ever-present at September's Gold Cup event, missing the 1982 meeting only because of his Silverstone Grand Prix crash. Conditions for the 1984 meeting were far from ideal and Barry found himself locked in battle around the tree-lined circuit with old sparring partner Mick Grant and rising stars David Griffith, Roger Burnett and Rob McElnea, all of them on identical RG500 Suzukis. Griffith won the first leg from Grant and Barry, but Sunday's 10-lap second leg saw Barry roll back the years and take the win, and with it the overall victory – the fourth time his name was added to the famous trophy.

CHAPTER 3
AWAY FROM THE TRACK

'I'm just an ordinary guy who makes his living out of riding a motorcycle in front of folks prepared to pay for the privilege of watching.' BARRY SHEENE

◄ Animals, and in particular cats, were a big passion of Barry's from an early age and at least half a dozen of them would roam the sprawling grounds of his Charlwood mansion. This one is enjoying the comfort of Barry's RG500 Suzuki.

AWAY FROM THE TRACK

People admire world champions, but they love world champions who do it all with a nod and a wink. Barry Sheene is still the antidote to the modern sports star with the manager, the PR and the portfolio of corporate diktats. What goes through your mind when you crash at high speed, he was once asked. 'Your arse,' he said.

Witty, intelligent, profane and profound, he had a style that coated his substance in gold dust. His legacy endures way beyond those who won more crowns, simply because of how he did it. Only Valentino Rossi has come close to matching his colour with his post-race stunts and late-night flourishes. Little wonder that Rossi, a nine-time world champion, regards Barry as a kindred spirit.

Podiums and near-death experiences were only part of it. His daughter, Sidonie, is now preserving these paternal traits. 'I'm definitely like my dad,' she said. 'My mum and brother are quite reserved, but I tend to say what I think straightaway. It's not necessarily a good thing, but the apple doesn't fall far from the tree when it comes to honesty and standing up for something – and he certainly didn't mind upsetting the applecart.'

◀ In 1978, Barry moved from a four-bedroom house in London's Putney to a 34-room, Elizabethan-style mansion house in the Surrey village of Charlwood – both Barry and Nixon the dog were completely at home.

Sheene cut through snobbery by being himself and having the gift of the gab.

Her brother, Freddie, says people often stop him to talk about his father. 'I was going through Customs recently and needed to sign some forms. When the officer saw my surname he just started going on about Dad. That sort of thing happens all the time.'

It may be hard to be objective from within the family, but Freddie probably nails the reason. 'He was quite cheeky and was always joking, but he was really friendly and remembered everyone's name. When you're in that scene and you show interest in your fans it goes a long way.'

He was the playboy prankster who flew a helicopter and crashed a Rolls-Royce. He was the schoolboy dropout with a degree in absenteeism, but he was the street-smart East End geezer, as happy in an oily garage as he was on a Monaco yacht. He cut through snobbery by being himself and having the gift of the gab, something he employed to crowd-pleasing effect on TV shows like *Parkinson* and *This is Your Life*. The latter, a prime-time career review, showed the respect in which he was held as Mike Hailwood flew in from New Zealand. 'I used to look over the fence at Hailwood surrounded by all these girls and think, "lucky bugger",' Barry said as he puffed away on a cigarette beside

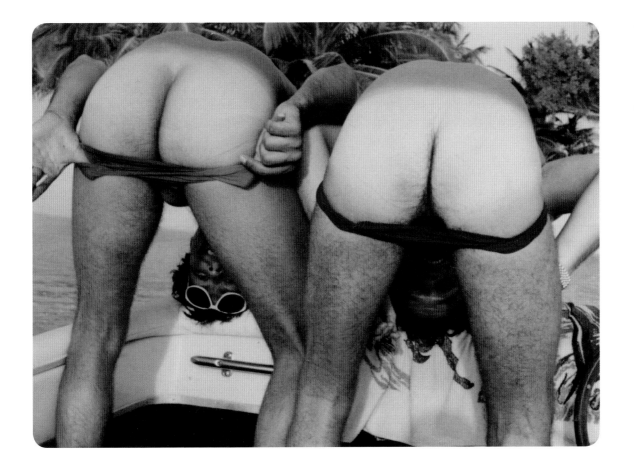

Barry was renowned for having a cheeky sense of humour – as he demonstrates here alongside fellow motorcycle racer Roberto Pietri, in Venezuela in 1980.

presenter Eamonn Andrews. His surgeon from Daytona flew in from the United States for that show. Steve Parrish shook his hand and grinned. When Giacomo Agostini, who had flown in from Italy, was announced as the last, star guest, Barry quipped: 'There'll be some fun tonight.'

The nights out were ribald subplots. Parrish recalled how he once dressed up in Barry's leathers and qualified for him, while Barry was smuggled out of the Mallory Park circuit in Leicestershire on the back seat of a Rolls-Royce.

'You had dog collars with your blood group on, so if I'd crashed they'd have put the wrong blood in me,' he said. 'It was just a wild time. It was so dangerous then and it

He was never truly the retiring type, so he was never going to swap his leathers for a pipe and slippers when his races were run.

seemed like someone died at every race, so you thought, "F*** it, let's have some fun." It's why Barry didn't encourage Freddie to get into motorbikes. No father wants to hang off a pit wall and see his son come past at 170mph.'

Another Parrish tale concerns a clandestine rescue mission to reclaim £250 of goods owed to Sheene's housekeeper by a former boyfriend. 'So we broke into a house wearing balaclavas and using a Rolls-Royce as a getaway,' he said.

Racing in that era was a mix of debauchery and deadly seriousness, but Barry's appeal crossed from the man in the street to the Beatles. 'It's artistic,' George Harrison said when asked what appealed to him about Barry.

There were certainly depths that were kept well-hidden. 'I didn't see him as being famous,' Sidonie said. 'He was just my dad. There was a completely different side to him other than his racing. Although I don't doubt he loved racing, it was a job. He did like the limelight, but he could also be private and there were days when he just wanted to hang out with his family. He was multilingual and encouraged me to learn languages. Behind the racing he had numerous different businesses.'

He was never truly the retiring type, so he was never going to swap his leathers for a pipe and slippers when his races were run. His popular appeal and ready smile made him a staple of TV light entertainment, and he had already shown his commercial nous with his Brut and Texaco sponsorship deals.

Synonymous with London and a British icon, Barry surprised some when he and Stephanie decamped to Australia in 1987. They moved to the Gold Coast after taking a trip there with George Harrison to watch the Australian Formula One Grand Prix in 1985. They enjoyed the location's laidback lifestyle and Barry found the hot weather was better for his mangled limbs.

In Australia he reinvented himself as a TV commentator. A penchant for forthright opinion swathed in entertaining vernacular impressed the bosses of Channel 9. And then he riled them with his enduring antics, whether it be hanging knickers on the studio wall or wearing a fake moustache.

Away from the track he developed a flourishing property empire. It now seems odd to think of a multi-millionaire playboy with a model wife and Surrey mansion as being the boy next door, but Barry carried it off. The hair never changed other than receding slightly in middle age. The perennial wardrobe involved jeans. According to the writer Stuart Barker, he once emptied a can of oil into a hotel swimming pool after a row with management about dinner dress codes.

He did not give up on racing, and indulged in trucks, saloon cars and classic events...

He did not give up on racing, and indulged in trucks, saloon cars and classic events, but by the late 1980s he was a father too. Sidonie and Freddie both went to boarding school in Australia and remember Barry as a strict father. Freddie recalled: 'If we borrowed money, he would need to know what it was for and we would have to perform some duty to pay him back. Mum was the soft one.'

However, this being Barry, his limits were idiosyncratic and Sidonie also remembers her father smuggling cigarettes to her at boarding school.

Freddie did not watch any of his father's races growing up and only truly appreciated his fame when he stepped out of the helicopter at the Phillip Island circuit in Australia to be met by a phalanx of photographers.

By then the helicopters were an integral part of the image. He bought his first three-seater while still on the Grand Prix circuit and blazed a trail for queue-jumping racers thereafter. His love of flying was such that, when he was dying from cancer, he made meticulous plans for the posthumous departure of his last, beloved chopper.

Sidonie says Barry was her 'go-to person for advice' and she was not alone. Barry's generosity to fledgling riders was highlighted by a letter he wrote to Mitsuo Itoh, a TT winner turned Suzuki top brass, about a young rider he had spotted. 'Mitsuo, I have every confidence in his ability to become a big fighter in the 500 GPs.' He urged a quick reply because he warned that others were also interested. 'His name is Michael Doohan. He is 22 years old.' Seven years later, when Michael had become Mick, he won the first of five successive 500cc titles.

Barry also became the mentor for another talented Australian called Chris Vermeulen, for whom he arranged rides in the British Supersport and Superstock Championships. After Barry's death, Vermeulen would repay the faith with second place in the 2005 World Superbike Championship and then victory at the 2007 French Grand Prix. He made sure that all his bikes bore the No. 7 in homage to his mentor.

Barry stuck with the No. 7 too, deeming it lucky despite his spills, a nod to how fate had twisted its rules for him. In many ways this was Barry, the rule-twister par excellence. He had been there, done it and bought the t-shirt, even if the logo did not belong to the manufacturer who had contracted him.

His reaction to the cancer was typical. 'A bloody pain in the backside,' was the blunt assessment. He refused to have chemotherapy because he had seen people 'destroyed' by the treatment, so he tried a diet of beetroot, Chinese cabbage and radish juice – a natural to his premature end in 2003 at the age of just 52.

◄ From 1977 to 1979 the San Carlos circuit in Venezuela hosted its nation's Grand Prix. Barry won the 500cc GP race in all three of those years – and looked forward to relaxing on the beach when the track activity was all over.

The trips abroad meant he and Stephanie could get away from the intense scrutiny of the UK tabloids and soak up the sun on the white, sandy beaches both in Venezuela and in Treasure Key in the Bahamas. For Barry, swimming trunks were optional!

'With Steph I'm the happiest I've ever been. I've got the best. She knows things about me that nobody else knows.'

BARRY SHEENE

◀ Water skiing became a huge hobby for Barry in the late 1970s and he was certainly very accomplished, whether it was in the warm climate of Venezuela or off the shore of Brighton. An owner of a 200bhp speedboat, he'd regularly fly down to the Sussex town in his helicopter and meet up with brother-in-law Paul Smart or good friend Steve Parrish.

Barry also enjoyed sea fishing and proudly shows off his prize catch in 1991.

▶ The 500cc World Championship calendar meant that Barry spent an awful lot of time during the year travelling around the world and aviation became a major interest as soon as he started to fly to the Grand Prix circuits abroad. Emergency visits to hospital prompted Barry to buy a helicopter of his own and he qualified as a helicopter pilot in record time in January 1982. The Hughes 500 was just one of the models he owned.

He was hooked from then on and flying became one of Barry's major passions and wherever he was in the world he took an interest in helicopters. He even made special provision for his beloved helicopter after his death.

▲ John Surtees, the only man ever to win World Championships on two wheels and four, arranged for Barry to have his first drive in a Formula One Grand Prix car at Brands Hatch in August 1977 during a private midweek session away from the glare of the media. With his car-mad pal and ex-Beatle George Harrison looking on, Sheene completed 70 laps of the short Indy circuit. Despite having faulty brakes, he came within 2.9 seconds of the lap record, but wasn't overly excited by the experience. 'It was no major problem to achieve that fast time,' he said later, 'and the experience, although enjoyable and requiring immense concentration, did not stimulate me to the point where I felt I just had to switch to four wheels.'

'… the experience, although enjoyable and requiring immense concentration, did not stimulate me to the point where I felt I just had to switch to four wheels.' BARRY SHEENE

'They asked me if I wanted a go [at truck racing] and I said "sure", it's right up my alley.'
BARRY SHEENE

▲ The first British Truck Grand Prix took place at Donington Park in 1984 and Barry was present because DAF trucks had sponsored him since 1980. Unlike close friend Steve Parrish, who went on to win seven European and British titles, Barry didn't take it, or the other truck races he entered seriously. He was a two-wheel man and truck racing was nothing more than light relief.

▲ Barry loved animals and at one time had as many as a dozen cats living in his Surrey home. Dogs and even lions cubs were on the receiving end of Barry's affections.

▲ On a visit to a Formula One Grand Prix at Long Beach, California, in April 1977, Barry met ex-Beatle George Harrison, and they immediately hit it off. Harrison was strolling round the garages when Barry spotted him and promptly introduced himself, and the sight of the two together at race meetings soon became a regular occurrence. Harrison was an avid motorcycle fan and a good friend of Barry's, and he later helped find sponsorship for Barry's close racing pal Steve Parrish. The friendship lasted right up until Harrison lost his own battle with cancer in November 2001.

▶ With his success on the track accompanied by friendships with the famous, it's little surprise that Barry featured in stories on the front and back of the daily newspapers. Indeed, Sheene the celebrity had numerous famous friends, including Monty Python's Eric Idle. It was George Harrison who introduced the two of them and such was the comedian's respect for the rider that in 1978 he recorded the song "Mr Sheene". This featured some questionable lyrics about Barry's big, red, throbbing 'riding machine'. It appeared on the B-side of the single "Ging Gang Goolie" and was credited to Rutles-offshoot duo Dirk and Stig.

' My family and friends are the best judge of me
but I would always describe myself as being
friendly and generally happy with life.' BARRY SHEENE

◄ Regarded as two of the most charismatic characters on the motor sport scene, Barry and Formula One's James Hunt often crossed paths and they became close friends. They shared sponsors, including Texaco and Brut, were press favourites and supported one another at each of their respective events. With a seemingly carefree attitude and desire to enjoy every minute of life, they were often described as 'playboys' and competing in two of the most dangerous sports in the world meant that the phrase 'live hard, play hard' certainly applied to them.

► With the American IndyCar Championship visiting Surfer's Paradise on an annual basis, Barry's TV work meant he got to spend time with avid motorsport fan and IndyCar team owner Paul Newman. Niki Lauda was another sportsman who held Barry in the utmost respect and regard for being a master of his profession.

'I like to consider myself a genuine, honest person and, because of that, I am entitled, just the same as anyone else, to speak my mind on subjects I feel strongly about.' BARRY SHEENE

▲ Barry relaxes by sitting on Kenny Roberts' 500cc Yamaha and having some fun in a go-kart in the paddock in the early 1980s.

▲ Barry's new life in Australia saw him reinvent himself as a leading commentator, incorporating both two and four wheel motorsport. Barry is joined on the grid in Melbourne by Stephanie and Sidonie for the 1999 Australian Formula One Grand Prix.

▶ Dad Franco and mum Iris joined their son and his family on the Gold Coast soon after he had emigrated to Australia. Barry designed and built his property to be big enough not only for his own needs but also to provide a home for Franco and Iris. Barry cherished his bike collection, which included both the 1976 and 1977 500cc World Championship winning machines, and he took great care in maintaining them. On this occasion, he is tending to the 1979 RG500 Suzuki.

'Dad was a mix of everything you could ask for in a father. He was strict but fair, fun but serious. My sister Sidonie and I both had a cheeky streak – I wonder where that came from!' FREDDIE SHEENE

◀ Such was his party-loving lifestyle in the 1970s few thought Barry would become a family man, but a decade later, he and Stephanie had two beautiful children. He married Stephanie in February 1984 and Sidonie was the first to arrive in November that year, Freddie joining her on the scene four years later. Barry had a very close relationship with Stephanie's son Roman and loved him like a son. He once said he would never live in Australia – because that was where some of his mechanics had come from (!) but a trip there with Beatle George Harrison in 1985 changed his mind, and the new family home on the Gold Coast of Australia was the perfect environment for raising a young family.

▲ By 1998 Barry and Stephanie had been settled on the Gold Coast for over a decade – and it's easy to see why. Their new home in Surfer's Paradise had all the trappings and luxuries befitting that of a successful sportsman and the laid-back lifestyle suited him well. 'One of the lovely things about living over here is that, having a young family, I can spend so much time with them,' he told Thames Television. 'There's no typical day for me, but I do get to spend a lot of time with my family.'

Ever since his crash at Daytona in 1975, Barry had noticed that his previously broken bones ached in the cold, wet conditions of the UK. Heat helped them and this was the main reason for emigrating. 'I didn't leave England because I didn't like it; I love England and had tremendous support there, but the reason I came to Australia was for health reasons and it's a great way to bring the family up.'

Barry's warmth of personality and down-to-earth nature meant that he struck up a number of great friendships throughout the course of his career.

▲ Two of his closest friends were Jeremy Paxton (left) and Jason Boland (right). They formed part of the infamous 'Squadron' and they used to hang out together on Australia's Gold Coast, waterskiing, flying helicopters and, once landed, enjoying the occasional drink!

▶ Julian Seddon was one Barry's oldest friends. They first met in the 1970s and worked together on a number of projects, including Barry's movie *Space Riders*. The film starred Barry and Stephanie as themselves, and told the story of Sheene's Silverstone crash and his pursuit of the World Championship.

◀ Alan Freedman was one Barry's best friends from his racedays. He owned the Brutus Jeans clothing company and sponsored Barry for a while.

▲ Barry didn't just move himself and all his family to Australia: his haul of trophies from his 15-year career came with him and it wasn't long before he had his own private collection of machinery assembled too. His pride and joy, the RT67 125cc Suzuki, had been sold at the end of 1971, but Barry bought it back in 1978, by which time he was a double world champion. He subsequently had it written into his contract that he could keep the bikes he raced and he took eight in total with him to Australia. A ninth machine, the big bore RG652cc Suzuki produced in 1977 for the home internationals, including the Transatlantic Trophy Races, was sent over by Suzuki GB and all of these bikes were carefully restored and maintained by Barry.

▶ Two legendary motorcycle world champions together: Barry shows Giacomo Agostini around his trophy room.

'Dad once rode the Transatlantic Suzuki 680 around the streets near home and everyone was looking and pointing at the bike.' BARRY SHEENE

▲ Sheene may have retired from racing in 1984, but he remained as busy as ever. Following his emigration to Australia in 1987, he was signed up by Channel 9 to co-present their motorsport coverage. Father Franco regularly accompanied Barry to events such as the Australian Formula One Grand Prix and it wasn't long before son Freddie, born in 1988, was by his Dad's side, even appearing with him on Channel 10's *RPM* motorsports programme.

▲ One of Australia's great motorcyclists was Wayne Gardner. He made his name in the UK in 1981 and for four years he battled regularly with Barry in the British Championships, firstly for Moriwaki and then Honda Britain. By 1984 he was a regular in the 500cc World Championship and when Barry retired at the end of 1984 Gardner was in the ascendancy. He became World Champion in 1987, retired in the 1992 season and then returned home to find a new career in the Australian Touring Car Championship and renew his acquaintance with Sheene.

▶ Even though he had retired from racing, Sheene kept a keen eye on the motorcycling talent in the country and he did all he could to help the aspirations of numerous riders, including Michael Doohan. In 1988, Barry approached Mitsuo Itoh, then Suzuki's racing boss and the only Japanese rider ever to have won at the Isle of Man TT, and wrote this letter encouraging Suzuki to sign the Queensland rider before other factories did. At this point, Doohan was already receiving help from Yamaha and Barry saw his potential as a future 500cc Grand Prix rider. Suzuki missed their opportunity, though. For the 1989 season Doohan signed with Honda, riding for them for his entire Grand Prix career and winning five consecutive 500cc World Championships between 1994 and 1998.

'His popularity in Britain is amazing. He's a household name in England despite retiring almost years ago. That's because his talent, personality and quick wit won the hearts of the people.'
MICK DOOHAN

2/2

DEAR MITSUO, RE OUR TELEPHONE CONVERSATION YESTERDAY 16TH, I WILL
NOW EXPLAIN ABOUT THIS YOUNG RIDER. HIS NAME IS MICHAEL DOOHAN
HE IS 22 YEARS OLD, HE STARTED RACING AUGUST 1985 ON RSV 500
PRODUCTION YAHAMA, HE FINISHED 1ST IN 1ST RACE, WHICH WAS 1 HOUR
ENDURANCE RACE, HIS 2ND RACE HE ALSO CAME 1ST PLACE. ATTACHED IS
A RESUME OF HIS RESULTS, YOU WILL SEE HE RACED IN SUGO IN 1987 AND
FINISHED 3RD. IT WAS HIS FIRST RACE ON A GP 750 c-c AND HE WAS
1st NON FACTORY MACHINE AT THE END OF 1987 YAMAHA AUSTRALIA WERE
ASKED BY FACTORY TO SIGN HIM WHICH THEY DID. 1988 HE HAS WON
ALMOST EVERY RACE IN AUSTRALIA INCLUDING BATHURST WHICH WAS IN THE
RAIN. HIS LAP TIMES HAVE BEEN FASTER THAN KEVIN MAGEE ON THE
SAME MACHINE. MITSUO I HAVE EVERY CONFIDENCE IN HIS ABILITY TO
BECOME A BIG FIGHTER IN 500 GP'S THE SAME ATTITUDE HE HAS LIKE
KEVIN SCHWANTZ. IF YOU ARE INTERESTED IN HIM HE CAN COME TO
JAPAN TO TEST. MITSUO I WOULD LIKE TO HELP HIM TO BE WITH SUZUKI
THE SAME WAY AS I DID KEVIN BECAUSE I BELIEVE YOU CAN HAVE TWO
GOOD RIDERS. PLEASE REPLY URGENTLY BECAUSE I KNOW YAMAHA ARE
VERY INTERESTED AND I THINK IT WOULD BE A MISTAKE TO LOOSE
THIS CHANCE.

BARRY SHEENE.

'I don't have any regrets, I did things the way I wanted to do them. The person that made up my mind for me was me.'
BARRY SHEENE

Stephanie would be by Barry's side at all of his race meetings and she immersed herself totally into her husband's profession, arming herself with a stopwatch and clipboard, and meticulously recording each and every one of Barry's practice or racing laps.

◄ Barry's final UK appearance came at the Goodwood Revival meeting in September 2002. Riding Fred Walmsley's 500cc Manx Norton, he finished a close second to 1987 500cc World Champion Wayne Gardner in the first of two races, but he got his revenge in the second by a slightly wider margin. More than 80,000 fans witnessed his final win, including good friend and former Formula One driver Austrian Gerhard Berger.

In July that year Barry rode the same 500cc Manx Norton in the classic races on the support programme at the British Grand Prix at Donington Park. Despite feeling unwell for some time, Barry wasn't going to let his good friend Walmsley or his UK fans down and he promptly won both races. On his return to Australia, he was diagnosed with cancer of the oesophagus and upper stomach, making the news public in a brief press release on 23 August. His final public appearance came at the Australian Grand Prix in October. He passed away on 10 March, 2003, aged 52.

▲ The absence of Barry at the 2003 Australian Grand Prix was felt strongly. A year before, he made his last visit to Phillip Island when, despite being already embroiled in his fight against cancer, he made sure he didn't miss a thing. The adopted Australian saw his life celebrated with a 700-strong convoy of bikes from Victoria, culminating in a full lap around the famous circuit. Five-times 500cc World Champion Michael Doohan also completed a lap on the same Manx Norton used by Barry to win his last race, and Stephanie was there too, bringing it to an end with an appreciative wave of the chequered flag.

◄ The new hero of racing, Valentino Rossi, won the MotoGP race in spectacular fashion, overcoming a 10-second penalty to claim the honours. He had his own celebration and memory of Barry pre-planned, carrying a flag bearing the No.7, made from a bed sheet 'borrowed' from the hotel – Barry would certainly have approved!

'Barry Sheene was not only one of the most brilliant motorcycle racers who ever lived, he was a lovely man too. He was brilliantly cheerful. He had a core of steel.' MURRAY WALKER

CHAPTER 4
BIKES AND RECORDS

'Don't wait for your ship to come in, swim out and meet the bloody thing!

BARRY SHEENE

◄ Some years may have been more successful than others, but the sight of Barry and Stephanie in the winner's enclosure after yet another victory was a familiar sight for over a decade.

BIKES

As comfortable on a 50cc two-stroke Kreidler as a 1000cc four-stroke Suzuki, Barry Sheene was nothing short of versatile during his racing career. During the early part of his career, he, like many others, rode wherever he could and on whatever he could, and earned success on a wide range of machinery – testament to his undoubted ability.

His favourite bike was the RT67 125cc Suzuki, which set him on the path to stardom. He sold it at the end of the 1971 season to fund the next stage of his career and bought it back in 1978. The cost was considerably more than what he'd sold it for, but he admitted he would have paid even more, such was its sentimental value.

When he started signing factory contracts, Barry had it written into his deal that he could keep the bikes he raced and his impressive collection was one to be admired.

◄ Barry's mechanic Ken Fletcher gives him and the RG500 Suzuki a push out of the pit lane at Donington Park at the beginning of 1983, the year he returned to Suzuki after three years at Yamaha.

125cc RT67 Suzuki

It took every penny Barry had to meet the £2000 price tag for Stuart Graham's ex-works 125cc RT67 Suzuki, made in 1967. A loan from his dad Franco made it possible for him to purchase it in 1970 and although three years old, the 10-speed, rotary valve two-stroke twin was still a very potent machine. Graham had finished third in the 1967 125cc World Championship and obtaining the bike was the biggest breakthrough in Barry's early career. Two days after buying the bike, he beat a star-studded field at Mallory Park and went on to finish second in the 1971 125cc World Championship, as well as taking two British titles.

1973 TR750 Suzuki

Although impressed by the speed of the TR750 Suzuki and the smaller 500cc version, Barry was horrified by the handling and he suggested that Suzuki commission ex-sidecar racer and chassis expert Colin Seeley to build a new frame. With the handling transformed, Barry won his first International title, the 1973 FIM Formula 750 Championship, as well as the 1973 MCN Superbike title.

1976 RG500 Suzuki

After three years of development, the 1976 version of the RG500 Suzuki was a born winner. Barry's works version – the only one on the grid – was lighter than the production version and powered by a different engine with a slightly different bore and stroke. It had a wider spread of power than the standard RG500, although Barry claimed it was no quicker. The results from 1976 suggest otherwise, though, as Barry swept to five wins from six starts to clinch the 500cc World Championship.

1977 RG500 Suzuki

Barry's 1977 Suzuki was a water-cooled two-stroke measuring 494cc and putting
out 108bhp. Pre-season Barry had been locked in negotiations with Suzuki and
there were rumours of him running his own Suzuki team, but he eventually
re-signed with Texaco Heron Suzuki to ride the latest version of the RG. Despite
increased competition, Barry won six races that year, the most famous of which
was the Belgian Grand Prix, where he lapped the 8.7-mile course in a record
average speed of 137.149mph. It remains the fastest ever lap recorded on any
circuit anywhere in the world.

1984 RG500 Suzuki

The RG500 Suzuki that Barry used for his final 500cc World Championship season in 1984 was fitted with Randy Mamola's ex-works XR45 motor, but he swapped the chassis for one made by Harris Performance. The engine proved to be slow, but the chassis expertise of Steve and Lester Harris meant that he had, arguably, the best handling machine on the grid. Variable head angles meant that Barry could alter the steering geometry of the bike from circuit to circuit, while the Harris brothers also fitted a variable rear suspension set-up. Barry's lack of horsepower put him at a major disadvantage, but the package offered by the Harris brothers gave him sweet handling that allowed him to claw back some of the deficit.

Arguably the most famous crash helmet in motorcycling, Barry's AGV helmet barely changed in design over the years save for sponsor's logos. In 1969, most riders had plain designs and basic colours, so Barry added the Donald Duck logo to the front to try and get some attention. It most certainly worked! You can also see where a hole was drilled into the chin guard to allow Barry to take in fluids and have one last puff on his cigarette before getting down to business.

'I chose that unusual [duck] sign because I reckoned it was so way-out that a lot of folks would have to take a second look.'
BARRY SHEENE

RECORDS

Having finished second in his first full season of racing in the 1969 125cc British Championship, Barry Sheene didn't take long to win his first title. Success came just a year later in 1970 while he was still a teenager. From that moment on, he never looked back with race wins and podiums each and every year both at home and abroad.

With his first Grand Prix victory coming in 1971, Barry went on to take race wins on a wide variety of circuits and on a wide range of machinery all around the world. His 15-year career was adorned with titles and championships as well as accolades off the circuit, his success being recognised by fellow racers, journalists and, of course, the British public.

TIMELINE

1950	Born on 11 September in London
1968	Makes racing debut at Brands Hatch on 17 March
1969	2nd 125cc British Championship (Bultaco)
1970	1st 125cc British Championship (Suzuki)
1970	2nd 250cc British Championship (Bultaco)
1970	Makes Grand Prix debut on 27th September at Barcelona
1971	Takes first GP win on 4 July in the 125cc race in Belgium
1971	2nd 125cc World Championship (Suzuki)
1971	1st 125cc British Championship (Suzuki)
1973	1st FIM Formula 750 Prize (Heron Suzuki)
1973	1st 500cc Shellsport Championship (Heron Suzuki)
1973	1st MCN Superbike Championship (Heron Suzuki)
1974	6th 500cc World Championship (Heron Suzuki)
1974	1st 500cc Shellsport Championship (Heron Suzuki)
1974	1st MCN Superbike Championship (Heron Suzuki)
1975	6th 500cc World Championship (Heron Suzuki)
1975	2nd FIM Formula 750 Prize (Heron Suzuki)
1976	1st 500cc World Championship (Texaco Heron Suzuki)
1976	1st 500cc Shellsport Championship (Texaco Heron Suzuki)
1976	1st MCN Superbike Championship (Texaco Heron Suzuki)
1977	1st 500cc World Championship (Texaco Heron Suzuki)
1977	1st 500cc Shellsport Championship (Texaco Heron Suzuki)
1977	1st MCN Superbike Championship (Texaco Heron Suzuki)
1978	2nd 500cc World Championship (Texaco Heron Suzuki)
1978	1st 500cc Shellsport Championship (Texaco Heron Suzuki)
1978	1st MCN Superbike Championship (Texaco Heron Suzuki)
1979	3rd 500cc World Championship (Texaco Heron Suzuki)
1980	15th 500cc World Championship (Akai Yamaha)
1981	4th 500cc World Championship (Akai Yamaha)
1982	4th= 500cc World Championship (John Player Special Yamaha)
1983	14th 500cc World Championship (Heron Suzuki)
1984	6th 500cc World Championship (Heron Suzuki)
1984	Makes final competitive outing 22 September at ITV World of Sport Superbike race
2002	1st and 1st in the Classic support races at the British Grand Prix
2002	1st and 2nd on a Manx Norton at the Goodwood Revival
2003	Passes away on 10 March, aged 52

GRAND PRIX SUMMARY

2 x World Championships	
102 x Grand Prix starts	
23 x Grand Prix wins	
52 x Grand Prix podiums	

GRAND PRIX WINS

1971	125cc Belgian Grand Prix (Spa-Francorchamps)
1971	50cc Czechoslovakian Grand Prix (Brno)
1971	125cc Swedish Grand Prix (Anderstorp)
1971	125cc Finnish Grand Prix (Imatra)
1975	500cc Dutch Grand Prix (Assen)
1975	500cc Swedish Grand Prix (Anderstorp)
1976	500cc French Grand Prix (Le Mans)
1976	500cc Austrian Grand Prix (Salzburgring)
1976	500cc Italian Grand Prix (Mugello)
1976	500cc Dutch Grand Prix (Assen)
1976	500cc Swedish Grand Prix (Anderstorp)
1977	500cc Venezuelan Grand Prix (San Carlos)
1977	500cc West German Grand Prix (Hockenheim)
1977	500cc Italian Grand Prix (Imola)
1977	500cc French Grand Prix (Paul Ricard)
1977	500cc Belgian Grand Prix (Spa-Francorchamps)
1977	500cc Swedish Grand Prix (Anderstorp)
1978	500cc Venezuelan Grand Prix (San Carlos)
1978	500cc Swedish Grand Prix (Karlskoga)
1979	500cc Venezuelan Grand Prix (San Carlos)
1979	500cc Swedish Grand Prix (Karlskoga)
1979	500cc French Grand Prix (Le Mans)
1981	500cc Swedish Grand Prix (Anderstorp)

◄ Barry's success in the 500cc World Championship saw him receive four FIM medals: two golds for his title-winning years of 1976 and 1977, silver for the runner-up spot in 1978 and bronze for third in 1979.

OTHER

Awarded an MBE in the Queen's New Year's Honours List – 1978	
Third, BBC Sports Personality of the Year – 1977	
Winner of the Seagrave Trophy – 1977, 1984	
Motor Cycle News Man of the Year – 1973, 1975, 1976, 1977 and 1979	
Winner of the International Gold Cup at Oliver's Mount, Scarborough – 1973, 1974, 1979, 1984	
Winner of the International Race of the Year at Mallory Park – 1974, 1975, 1978	

BONES BROKEN DURING RACING CAREER

Toes	3x Left / 4x Right
Left Ankle	Once
Right Ankle	4 Times
Left Tibia and Fibula	Once
Right Tibia and Fibula	Twice
Left Femur	Once
Heelbone	Once
Vertebrae	Twelve
Ribs	4x Left / 5x Right
Split Kidney	Once
Collarbone	3x Left / 4x Right
Right Forearm	Once
Wrist	4x Left / 1x Right
Metacarpals	4x Left
Knuckles	4x Left
Fingers	4x Left
Amputated Left Little Finger	

TEAMS AND BIKES

1968–1969

TS 125cc Bultaco (Sheene Racing)

TS 250cc Bultaco (Sheene Racing)

TS 350cc Bultaco (Sheene Racing)

1970–1971

50cc Van Veen Kreidler (Kreidler Racing)

TS 125cc Bultaco (Sheene Racing)

TS 250cc Bultaco (Sheene Racing)

TS 350cc Bultaco (Sheene Racing)

RT67 125cc Suzuki (Sheene Racing)

TD 250cc Yamaha (Gerard Brown)

250cc Derbi (Derbi Racing)

T20 250cc Suzuki (Crooks Racing)

350cc Yamsel (John Cooper Racing)

TR500 Suzuki (Sheene Racing)

500cc Kawasaki Mach 1

750cc Norton Commando (Gus Kuhn Racing)

1972

250cc TZ Yamaha (Sonauto Yamaha)

350cc TZ Yamaha (Sonauto Yamaha)

1973

TR 500cc Suzuki (Suzuki GB)

TR 750cc Suzuki (Suzuki GB)

1974–75

RG 500cc Suzuki (Suzuki GB)

TR 750cc Suzuki (Suzuki GB)

1976

RG 500cc Suzuki (Texaco Heron/Suzuki GB)

RG 535cc Suzuki (Texaco Heron/Suzuki GB)

RG 750cc Suzuki (Texaco Heron/Suzuki GB)

1977–1979

RG 500cc Suzuki (Texaco Heron/Suzuki GB)

RG 652cc Suzuki (Texaco Heron/Suzuki GB)

GS 1000cc Suzuki (Paul Dunstall Racing – 1979 only)

1980–1981

OW54 & OW60 TZ 500cc Yamaha (Akai Yamaha/Barry Sheene Racing)

TZ 750cc Yamaha (Akai Yamaha/Barry Sheene Racing)

1982

OW60 TZ 500cc Yamaha (John Player Special/Barry Sheene Racing)

1983–1984

RG 500cc Suzuki (Heron Suzuki GB)

XR69 1000cc Suzuki (Heron Suzuki GB)

INDEX

CREDITS

The publishers would like to thank the following sources for their kind permission to reproduce the pictures in this book.

Estate of Barry Sheene: 6, 9, 13, 15, 16, 21, 23, 24, 26-27, 28, 29 bl & br, 30, 34, 35, 36-37, 38-39, 41, 47, 49, 56, 60, 65, 66, 70, 80, 81, 82, 83, 84-85, 86, 90, 91, 92, 100, 104, 105, 112 r, 113, 118, 119, 132, 135, 138, 139, 146, 148, 149, 152, 153, 166, 168, 171, 176, 177, 178, 179, 180, 182, 183, 184 t, 185, 186, 187, 189, 190, 191, 192, 193 tl, 193, ml, 193 bl, 194, 195, 196, 197, 198, 199, 200, 201, 202, 216, 217, 220, 223

Original photography and archival image processing by Rod Morris

Dave Dyer / F1 Photographs: 193 r

Don Morley: 4, 109, 110-111, 141, 161

FremantleMedia: 68-69

Getty Images 19, 29 t, 31, 43, 46, 71, 76-77, 79, 106-107, 108, 112 l, 114, 115, 121, 127b, 128-129, 130, 131, 133, 134, 144, 145, 159, 162-163, 206, 207, 208, 210

Gerard Kampen: 48, 150, 165

Jasin Boland: 211, 212, 213, 214, 215

LAT Photographic: 10-11

MirrorPix: 50-51, 52, 53, 73, 96, 97, 102, 103, 136, 142, 154, 155, 158, 181, 184 b

Mortons Archive: 32, 40, 42, 44-45, 74-75, 88-89, 99, 101, 120, 122-123, 147

Phil Wain Family Archive: 137, 140, 143, 160

Press Association: 54, 78, 87, 157 164, 224

Richard Francis / Actionplus: 151

Suzuki GB: 93, 94–95, 116, 124–125, 126, 127 b

www.sutton-images.com: 188, 205

Every effort has been made to acknowledge correctly and contact the source and/ or copyright holder of each picture and Bloomsbury apologizes for any unintentional errors or omissions that will be corrected in future editions of this book.

Bloomsbury would like to thank the Estate of Barry Sheene's management team, Santara Group (www.santaragroup.com), for their support and work on this book.

Records compiled by Phil Wain

▲ Race number '7' will forever be associated with Barry Sheene. It adorned his bike, helmet and leathers from 1974 to 1984, and Sheene continued to use the number when he was reigning world champion even though he was entitled to ride as No.1.

Barry Sheene 1950–2003

Barry's impact on motorcycle racing in the UK was huge and is still talked about to this day. No one did as much for the sport, on or off the track, and that he's still spoken about so much tells its own tale. Other riders may have won more Grands Prix and more world titles, but his personality, charisma and willingness to speak his mind benefited not just himself, but every motorcycle racer since.